Between Remembering and Forgetting

Between Remembering and Forgetting

The spiritual dimensions of dementia

Edited by
James Woodward

mowbray

Published by Mowbray a Continuum imprint
The Tower Building, 11 York Road, London, SE1 7NX
80 Maiden Lane, Suite 704, New York, NY 10038

www.continuumbooks.com

First published 2010

British Library Cataloguing-in-Publication Data
A catalogue record for this book is available from the British Library.

ISBN: 978–1–4411–3114–0

Designed and typeset by Kenneth Burnley, Wirral, Cheshire
Printed and bound in Great Britain by the MPG Books Group

Contents

Introduction

For over a decade I was privileged to work alongside older people in the Foundation of Lady Katherine Leveson. In their humanity and frailty they enriched my life and growth. In this work I was concerned that those of us who organized the provision of housing and care to older people should think and reflect as well as deliver care. This was behind the establishment of the Leveson Centre for the Study of Ageing, Spirituality and Social Policy. I wanted the culture of the charity to be a place of learning and reflection. It was our hope that the Centre would bring people together from across the professions to learn from each other and discover ways of improving practice.

My own ministry had been much influenced by a year spent at St Christopher's Hospice in south London under the leadership of Dame Cicely Saunders. We kept in touch and she took some pleasure in my commitment to work among older people. Some months before she died, she wrote and told me that if she were to tackle a health need in the twenty-first century, it would be dementia care that would attract her energy (as cancer and palliative care had done decades earlier). Inspired by this challenge, the Centre embarked upon a number of conferences which aimed to explore dementia, dementia care provision and especially the spiritual aspects of this work.

This book offers the fruit of some of that work. I have gathered together a number of papers given at our seminars in order to stimulate and inform the reader about some of the challenges that face us as a society when we consider the nature of dementia and its effects on us all.

As a regular reviewer of books, I have often commented on the many problems of collections of essays. They are inevitably and invariably uneven, and making the connections between the chapters can sometimes be rather a challenge. However, as the editor of this collection of essays, I believe that they offer something particularly distinctive and helpful to one of the major challenges facing us today. The pieces here are made particularly unique because the majority of writers are practitioners rather than theorists. I ask that the reader exercise some patience in the engagement with such variety of style.

There are twelve pieces. In all of them the voice of the person living with dementia is never very difficult to hear. Chapter 1 offers a basic introduction to how we might understand dementia. We are reminded that precise definitions are difficult to achieve because of the nature of the disease. The next two chapters offer a brief introduction to some of the pastoral and spiritual needs of people with dementia. The reader will see that here and throughout the book the focus is on the person and how we might better understand how dementia shapes and mis-shapes the nature of a person. At the heart of present health-care practice is the principle that each person is and always remains an individual from birth to death. Every moment and challenge demands that we offer dignity and respect. Both Brian Allen and Judith Allford remind us that every person is entitled to the best of care that is tailored to suit their individual needs. Theologically we are reminded of a basic affirmation of Christianity: that every person is created uniquely and in the image of God. We should be ashamed, therefore, if we or our systems of care fail to see those who live with dementia as anything other than the person whom God created. In this respect this book has inevitable political and social dimensions – each of the essays makes its reader aware of the gaps both in our understanding of dementia but also in the lack of imaginative and resourced care. Read carefully the moving story of Judith Allford and together we might ask what would have needed to be different in order for our responses to be more spiritually person focused?

In the next four chapters we explore with skilled practitioners what quality of life means for people with dementia. In Chapter 4, Margaret Anne Tibbs discusses what the elements are for good care. Here she considers the important issue of communication with people with dementia and explores ways in which faith survives or fails to survive under this assault on the self. In Chapter 5, John Killick – a creative pioneer – shows us how it is possible to establish and maintain meaningful relationships with people living with dementia. He illustrates this with moving poems from people whom he has interviewed. In Chapter 6, Gaynor Hammond introduces us to the role of reminiscence in helping older people with dementia retain their personhood. She describes the idea of the Memory Box which contains people's personal mementos and helps them to retain their identity. In Chapter 7, Sally Knocker builds upon our developing understanding of what the needs of older people with dementia are by suggesting that time, attention, human contact, conversation and a friendly smile are some of the most important gifts we can offer. She looks at the work of Tom Kitwood in this area and concludes that this should be an important ministry for churches.

In the next section, a very practical essay grounded in the wise experience of practice by Patricia Higgins and Richard Allen, offers principles to be followed when planning a service of worship. It takes us comprehensively through a range of practical considerations. One is left feeling, perhaps, that all worship ought to be as sensitively and creatively planned and celebrated. We have much to learn from this piece about how our spiritual needs are expressed and met in worship.

One of the main challenges facing religion in the twenty-first century is how we might talk about our encounter with God. It is often the poet who helps us to gain a deeper sense of the encounter as often both strange and intractable. In a strange land between remembering and forgetting, these essays bear testimony to the distressing reality of dementia and remind us that it is becoming an increasingly common experience across the Western world. This is particularly problematic and soul-crushing for those who sit and watch as loved ones and carers. The experience for many can be a soul-crushing and painful struggle – a long death as the person that we knew becomes slowly unrecognizable even to themself.

In the final section we consider how a spiritual approach to the person with dementia might empower us to work together for a good death. The reader should note the precious dignity that all these four writers aim to promote. These pieces are not only good examples of what is or might be a good death, but also how all human beings ought to be treated in their fragility and need. In Chapter 9, Katherine Froggatt writes about the difficulties involved in applying the concept of palliative care or end-of-life care to people living with dementia, who may have limited awareness of what is happening and for whom the dying process may extend over several years. The next chapter, written by a doctor, Adrian Treloar, argues that dignity is always preserved when people are given choice. Here he explores the option of continuing to care for a person with dementia at home until the end. He offers case studies where it has been done successfully and explores the conditions which are required to make it possible. In Chapter 11, Margaret Goodall suggests that the search for meaning is the overriding spiritual need of people living with dementia as they approach the end of life. And finally, in Chapter 12, Beatrice Godwin draws our thoughts together in a reflection on how we might achieve a good death in dementia. This essay draws us back to people and practice, and from a spiritual perspective we note again that for people living with dementia, their self-esteem, well-being and in the end their continuing personhood may depend not so much upon the progression of the disease as upon the attitudes of those around them.

The person living with dementia can become elusive and even meaningless. There are profound theological implications of this. These essays are relevant to all of us who want to think about the day-to-day challenge of living wondering about any spiritual coherence or even God-given coherence in the experience.

What we face in all of this is how we choose to describe or understand human experience. In this sense, this book is only a modest start to a conversation about human life, age and diminishment that must take place among all kinds of people who want to see values other than independence, success, activity and material comfort dominate our demanding lives.

Many of the writers here ask that we seek an alternative paradigm which understands dementia as at least partly to do with the way a person is perceived, understood and treated. Kitwood[1] has been a pioneer in challenging the increasing marginalization, disempowerment and isolation of people living with dementia. The problem is not simply a malfunction in the person's brain, but a malfunction in the philosophy and underpinnings of society's understandings of personhood.

So the spiritual challenge of living in the land between remembering and forgetting is about relationships, shared meanings and the hope that comes from challenging imprisoning expectations, assumptions and presuppositions. We need to be reflective and wise – engaging with the spiritual as a key which can unlock both how we understand human beings and their potential, and respond in the building up of relationships and therefore community.

I hope that these essays offer a contribution to this debate.

James Woodward
The College of St George, Windsor Castle

Note

1 Kitwood, T., *Dementia Reconsidered*, Open University Press, 1997.

Chapter 1

What is Dementia?

KATE READ

In'this chapter the Executive Director of Dementia Plus offers a basic intro-duction to how we might understand dementia. We are reminded that precise definitions are difficult to achieve because of the nature of the disease. The term 'dementia' is something of a blanket word used to describe a number of disorders associated with the loss of brain functions that are progressive and, to date, irreversible. Currently, the Alzheimer's Society estimates that there are something in excess of 750,000 people in the UK who live with one or more of over 100 types of dementia. Implicit in these statistics and descriptions is the need for early diagnosis and treatment. The reader needs to bear in mind that it is invariably associated with older age, early symptoms tend to be attributed to the ageing process, or confused with stress or depression. We are also chal-lenged to consider the shape of good care practice.

Dementia is a condition very strongly associated with late life, and in par-ticular people aged over 80. While approximately 1 per cent of people over 65 suffer from dementia, the likelihood rises as people age, with 24 per cent of people over 85 having dementia. But in working with older people it is important to remember that the converse is true: 99 per cent of people over 65 do *not* have dementia, and even in the very oldest cohorts over three-quarters do not have dementia.

But what is dementia? In 1982 the Royal College of Physicians defined it thus:

The acquired global impairment of higher cortical functions including memory, the capacity to solve the problems of day-to-day living, the performance of learned perceptuo-motor skills, the correct use of social skills and the control of emotional reactions, in the absence of gross clouding of consciousness. The condition is often irreversible and progressive.

So it is something that usually affects memory, in particular of recent events. Do not assume people remember nothing; often important earlier memories are retained. It can affect intellect. New learning is difficult, thinking may be slower and judgement less good, but good signage and prompts can help. Mood can be affected. Some people can become anxious, depressed or agitated; likewise some people's behaviour changes and a previously mild-mannered person can become angry or behave with uncharacteristic disinhibition, but good care and attention to the person's well-being help.

However, it must be emphasized that no two people experience dementia in quite the same way – it is a very individual experience. Also, the experience changes for the person over time, so it is important to keep a watching brief and respond as their needs change. Carers and supporters should be aware that the person's memory and skills can fluctuate from day to day. A familiar example is that of carers who tell of frustrating times trying to dress someone who has always been able to dress unaided but one day loses a step in the process and can no longer do it – but then later in the week can again dress perfectly. Carers who do not understand dementia can find themselves wondering if the person was trying to wind them up! They were not; it is a facet of the way dementia manifests itself that such variations can occur.

Generally the pattern of dementia over several years is one of declining cognition, emotions and behaviours which carers can find increasingly challenging, alongside increased physical difficulties.

What is it that makes us the people we are? I believe that the experiences throughout our lifetime are fundamental in making us into the people we have become. The early memories: first pet, Mum bringing brother or sister back from hospital, our first day at school, first star, first detention (or worse), first pay cheque, first boyfriend, subsequent boyfriends, getting married, illness, bereavement. All these and many, many more memories have formed us. Part of our memory and our ability to recall these images contributes to our sense of self, including both the wonderful and the sad moments.

I picture my memory as hundreds of windows through which I can look back to these moments. Many of them interconnect, leading me on or back to other moments or people remembered. But what happens when the view through one of those windows is blank? In truth we all have those moments – often when we are stressed or tired, worrying about something or just not concentrating. The face is familiar but the name has gone temporarily. This is *not* dementia, but merely a natural reaction to the pace of life.

But what of the occasion when your husband asks you to post a letter, and when you get home again you cannot even remember he asked you – the letter is still there in the bag! Even more worrying when it is there in front of you, you do not recognize it, and are still adamant you have *never* seen it before. If that becomes a regular pattern, it is certainly worth seeking advice. Most people who develop dementia or who live with someone with dementia will say that it was not the first incident that alerted them but a repeated pattern of difficulties.

And certainly experienced practitioners will be looking for that pattern, the history of memory problems developing rather than a single incident. However, note that if there is a sudden decline over a matter of a day or two then medical help should be sought as a priority because a rapid onset of memory problems can often be an indication of physical illness, for example severe infection, which can be treated and needs to be treated. The treatment will then alleviate the memory problems too.

One of the facets of memory that we all use most of the time is the power of association. Try to remember quickly a list of random letters, for example:

GFMS   SDNO   CZPA   PVTE   VRXI   AQBM

Most people find that challenging. But if given the following list of the same number of letters, most people can remember them more easily:

REME   PDSA   WRAF   WABC   BRMB   RSPB

Why is that? The key lies with association. The second list is easier to remember because the letters are meaningful – most people know of PDSA as the Peoples' Dispensary for Sick Animals, so the letters are meaningful, and once the link is made they are easier to remember. Indeed, some people remember by making a further link, perhaps visualizing a sick pet to reinforce the memory.

The difficulties start arising when it is not one or two blank windows out of the hundreds of memories or items of knowledge. The real problems start when, because one window is blank, there is no link to the next window, and so, over a period of time a whole wall of our memory, which was full of images, becomes filled with holes – and the final picture can look increasingly blank and therefore bleak.

But this is where good care really comes into its own. If what is happening in the present links to a surviving memory which is positive, then the person is more likely to be relaxed and content. If many windows are blank and the present activity is unpleasant or connecting back to a worry or negative experience, the person is far more likely to be anxious or even angry and frustrated. Recognizing these cues, acknowledging them and working with them to try to achieve the optimum well-being for the person, is one of the fundamentals of person-centred care.

Even a person with advanced dementia will have times of insight and understanding. John Killick in *Communication and the Care of People with Dementia* relates some of his conversations with a lady named Alice who was living in a nursing home. Although her dementia was considerable, she had insight into what was happening to her and could express it with great dignity and poetry: 'The brilliance of my brain has slipped away when I wasn't looking.'

Conversations with Alice also provided a salutary reminder of the impact of poor care practice. In particular, Alice's plea below emphasizes the interplay of dementia and poor practice, which together can close many of the windows in a person's memory. This then insidiously takes away from them the facets of their history and experience which make them the individual personality they are.

Are you a person who could swing it for me with the authorities? I want you to ask them a question for me: Would they please give me back my personality?

Good care practice can do much to address such situations, and this is one of our challenges.

For further information

Killick, J. and Allan, K., *Communication and the Care of People with Dementia*, Open University Press, 2001.

For web-based resources see:

www.alzheimers.org.uk;
www.nhs.uk/Dementia;
www.alzheimers-research.org.uk.

SECTION 1

The Pastoral and Spiritual Needs of People with Dementia

Chapter 2

Remembering the Cost –
A Theological Reflection

BRIAN ALLEN

Brian Allen brings many years of experience as chaplain to this reflective piece on the nature and challenge of dementia. Grounded in practice, the chapter asks its readers to consider the person amidst the terror of change and loss. It is a mark of the health of spiritual communities that they have the compassion to invest time with vulnerable people and allow them to be teachers of a deeper theology of care and community. We need to embrace the cost of dementia so that it can unlock a profounder sense of what is precious about personhood.

When considering the pastoral care of those living with dementia, the following distinctions may be helpful:

Pastoral care

For many practitioners of care, this is a concept that is perhaps best understood instinctively, in the doing rather than the thinking about. In his 1985 book *Paid to Care?*, Alistair V. Campbell suggests that pastoral care is primarily concerned with the experience of love, both received and given. Since the term 'pastoral' originates in the action of shepherds caring for their flock (and is a widely used Christian metaphor for the relationship between God and his creation), Campbell's suggestion instinctively feels like it has some validity.

Moreover, observation of the manner in which many care-givers (be they doctors, nurses, health-care assistants, family members and friends, even chaplains) interact with those living with dementia, Campbell's emphasis on an encounter of mutual love would seem to be a demonstrably accurate and useful starting point.

Spiritual care

If much energy has been expended over the years in defining pastoral care, the past decade has seen a burgeoning in spiritualities at the expense of religion, certainly of the organized kind. The term 'spirituality' has been appropriated by almost every individual or group that perceives itself to be involved in the search for the meaning of life. Many understand spiritual care primarily to be concerned with searching for an answer to the question:

'In my current state of health, just who am I?'

Buried in this apparently simple question lie notions of identity, some awareness of a relationship with God or a life force, the context of one's own and other people's environments, and a feeling that life ought to have both meaning and purpose. Experience suggests that perceptions of individual identities depend on many factors and vary throughout life. So the question is particularly relevant for those who live with dementia, in view of the very considerable life changes that are being experienced.

Religious care

This is perhaps the easiest of the three terms on which to gain a general level of consensus. The very word 'religious' establishes boundaries and presupposes a degree of faith, albeit without identifying any particular group affiliation. We might therefore define religious care as

. . . the provision of formal and informal opportunities that enable patients, users, carers and staff to express their faith and practise their religion.

Living with dementia

For people with dementia, enhancing their feeling of well-being at a time of great change is perhaps the most important goal. High quality clinical care can only be achieved when each individual is viewed as a whole person, valued for whom they are and not primarily what they are capable of doing. Identifying individual needs in all aspects of life is thus of paramount importance.

Pastoral care is primarily expressed through meeting physical and emotional needs and is the starting point of Campbell's continuing dialogue of love. However, identifying spiritual and religious needs, still more facilitating their expression as an integral part of holistic care, is often overlooked.

Ordinarily, most people meet their spiritual and religious needs by belonging to a particular faith group and meeting periodically or regularly for ritual acts of religious expression. Those over 70 years of age come from a generation for whom regular attendance at church, synagogue, temple or mosque was a far more common part of everyday life than it is for the present generation. For many from within a Christian context, religious education at school and attendance at Sunday School would have been formative experiences in equipping them for a life that carried a faith dimension.

A story remembered

Gordon has told his story many times now, but there was a time when no one was listening to what he was saying. The turning-point was when, at his wits' end, he told his GP that he could cope no longer and was prepared to kill himself. The response was to refer him for psychiatric assessment, which duly took place. This was when doctors recognized that what Gordon could no longer cope with was caring unaided for Janet, his wife, who by then was living in the moderate to severe stages of dementia. Having shared a lifetime of work and family homemaking together, Janet had gradually become unable to recognize people, fulfil those daily functions which she had been used to carrying out, and communicate with her own family and friends in a way they could understand. This diagnosis was the first step to her receiving the level of care that was available in a nursing home which both welcomed and supported Gordon's continued involvement with the care it was recognized that Janet needed.

Gordon told me his story, which we then shared with the nursing home staff. This was followed by Janet's consultant asking Gordon to address medical students, many of whom have made it clear that not only have they found Gordon's story very moving but also vital in alerting them to the importance of listening to patients' and carers' stories; this would help them make an early diagnosis so that people with dementia and their carers may receive the assistance they require. Gordon's wife has since died, but he continues to keep in touch with the nursing home, address medical students regularly and volunteer with remarkable commitment at the local carers' centre.[1]

Gordon's story is by no means unique, but it highlights the way in which dementia can impact not only on the sufferer but also on others immediately involved. Ignorance and stigma, as much if not more than the process of the disease itself, can often leave people on their own, with devastating consequences. It is then vital to receive an appropriate diagnosis so as to be able to access the help needed.

Dementia challenges us on many levels, from social policy to underlying philosophical questions about the nature of personhood, from theological dilemmas to the practice of providing good quality care for everyone affected.

Loss is common to all forms of dementia and affects carers as well as sufferers, who often experience loss of relationship, an anticipated future and social contact as the demands of caring can lead to isolation. Indeed, dementia has been called the 'long bereavement'[2] where the emotional pain associated with grief is compounded by the disease process and societal attitudes to it.

Another discourse, which occurs in popular literature, can be termed 'sentimental', for it seldom reaches beyond saying, 'Isn't it a pity this is the way things are?'

Neither the technical nor the sentimental approaches is adequate, for they fail to demonstrate a direct concern for the sufferer's subjectivity. This is hard, for no one returns to tell us what it is like (unlike, say, people who experience psychotic episodes for depression or schizophrenia). However, some sufferers have an awareness which they are able to articulate, at least in the early stages of the disease, and others have done much to give voice to sufferers' experience, for example the poet John Killick.[3] However, the process of the disease is particular to each person, the determinants imprecise, and confirmation of any clinical diagnosis normally only possible post mortem.

Tom Kitwood, an academic moral psychologist who pioneered the work of the Dementia Group at Bradford University, argued for a person-centred approach to the care of people with dementia, perhaps better described as people whose mental powers are diminishing.[4]

Martin Buber's classic *I and Thou* influenced much of Kitwood's promotion of the new culture of dementia care which sees people with dementia as primarily persons, and persons in relationship. Characteristically Hebraic, as indeed it is of the Judaeo-Christian tradition, Buber describes life as dialogue: in the beginning is relationship. Buber points to the irreducibility of the personal and of the communion between persons, suggesting that the locus of meaning is in the encounter, the communication of the one with the Other. 'In the beginning and in the end is relationship, which can never be transcended or absorbed – even in God. There is the closest possible mystical unity between I and Thou, but always it is a mysticism of love, which insists upon and respects the non-identity of the other.'[5] The same point has been made elsewhere, of course, and is particularly pertinent in relation to discussions about the personhood of people with dementia, not least given its prevalence.

Maintaining a positive regard for the person with dementia requires much of the carer. Both are themselves in relation to the other. Faith Gibson has questioned the demands made upon carers by the high standards set by Buber's concept of 'dialogical living',[6] as interpreted and applied by Kitwood and others. Her conclusion is, however, that we can do nothing less. To ignore one person's diminishment is to diminish us all. Furthermore, it should be recognized that it is often the case that people with dementia require much of others – but also show others much about the range of human communication and therefore much of what it is to be human. If we are to understand the human experience of dementia, it is essential to see all aspects of personhood in relational terms.

Kitwood's work focused on confronting what he termed the 'malignant social psychology' which operates to the detriment of people with dementia so much that they are regarded as less than persons. Kitwood lists at least ten negatives, including such attitudes and practices as infantilization, labelling, outpacing and objectification, all of which detract from the possibilities of affirming personhood and thus deprive a person of the opportunity to realize their potential.

This person-centred approach proposes that the sufferer is not regarded as a disease-bearer but rather as a person who is suffering or experiencing disability that is terminally progressive. It does not deny the reality of the disease but focuses more on a person's abilities than their disabilities. This approach lays stress on the identity of personhood as experience in place and community.

Eileen Shamy pioneered a Christian ministry in New Zealand specifically with and for people with dementia and their carers.[7] She commented that to ask a Maori person what had happened to their identity or their memory was to make a category mistake. Both their identity and memory were understood to reside in the group, the community, the place and even the very earth. They are not the possession of the individual; personal identity lives in the place and the community rather than in the mere individual.

Steven Rose[8] offers different models of the brain's activity in storing memory through life. One vivid image is of a manic homebuilder constantly removing house bricks and replacing them with new ones. A more static and apparently less accurate image is of a tape cassette where retrieval is achieved at the press of the rewind button followed by play, and you are back listening to what you were listening to beforehand. This is an inadequate image because, Rose argues, it is not dynamic. The human brain is part of a living organism, living in a world of meaning and not simply information.

Where memory is problematic, not least for guaranteeing continuity, being remembered by God in the land of forgetfulness (Psalm 88.12) is not only a statement of faith but also one which opens up the possibilities for the location of memory. Rather than limited by definition as a function of the individual, it is seen as that which resides in community, tradition and place, and so is not entirely dependent on any one individual's level of cognitive function. Clearly the practice of communities observing ritual and a special sense of place or sacred space as a way of 're-membering' is not the monopoly of any one tradition. Belonging to and being remembered by both Church and society are particularly significant themes in the instance of people with dementia.

The Church of England's *Ageing*, a report from the Board for Social Responsibility, refers to Hugo Petzch's study of societal attitudes to people with dementia, in which he described three models. These are biblical models which arise out of reflecting upon times spent working among people suffering from dementia. The 'scapegoat' model (Leviticus 16) responds to some of the least favourable attitudes where the need to distance oneself from the victim and to avoid any fear of contamination by association are both present. Those who are put out of sight bear the burden of the guilt of society for the breakdown in relationships. The image of the suffering servant provides the second model, where the servant's plight and the onlookers' responses (Isaiah 53.2b–3, 4) speak of the collective nature of the problem. The restoration of broken relationships can begin when we recognize that our attitudes play a part in distancing others, including people with dementia. Some health service and church work operates in this way. Reports raise issues that all too often lead to 'informed inertia'. High-dependency nursing may concentrate on practical and physical tasks alone, and people with dementia become valuable objects as potential brain tissue donors to assist in all-age psychiatry. Petzch argued that these two models are not exclusive, nor are they definitive by any means. People can often be traced to move in and out of both. His third model is to establish a more appropriate response to the problem of our relationship with people whose cognitive functioning is disturbed and diminishing. This draws upon the New Testament account of the Gadarene demoniac (Luke 8) where the emphasis is upon someone rejected by society who is called by name, offered unconditional acceptance (i.e. not subjected to the 'malignant social psychology' of infantilization, outpacing, objectification and so on), and the saving act that culminates in the person's restoration to society. Here Petzch stressed that the will to restore the person is prerequisite. Unconditional acceptance will bring concern for the plight of sufferers who are otherwise rejected; and the will and means to alleviate the suffering, even if at present it is incurable, can follow.

These models are, of course, provisional but are consistent with much of the history of recent care of people with dementia (especially severe dementia) and experiences to which some carers, both relatives and professionals, bear witness. Some memorable images against which to test attitudes are present in Tony Harrison's *Black Daisies for a Bride*,[9] a television documentary drama in which people with dementia play themselves and come alive both as persons with a past and as persons in the present with abilities. These abilities are often masked by neglect or misunderstanding of their behaviour which can always be regarded as communicating a meaningful message.

Spiritual and pastoral care of people with dementia can be said to be based upon an unconditional person-centred approach, as the foundation for a ministry centred on the personhood shared with Christ. However, much of the Western tradition has a view of 'persons' that sees them as defined by function and rationality, and thus dysfunction and irrationality are indicators of non/sub persons. This appears as a comment on society itself unable to cope with being confronted by apparent weakness and dependence – seeing it as meaninglessness and failure. Such attitudes, often born out of fear, can achieve moral and political acceptability so that it is even possible to murder those whose brains do not function well and to call this action 'euthanasia'. This refers, of course, to the murder of thousands of mental hospital patients carried out in Nazi Germany by doctors. The German psychiatrist Alfred Hoche used the word '*Ballastexistenzen*' (human ballast) to apply to such people – people you could dispose of without society losing anything essential. This is blasphemy against the Creator because they are inseparably connected to others through that creation which gives those others apparently well-functioning brains. And so a theology of creation includes here the concept of purposeful creativity (lovingly wrought) in which deviation is a natural part of the process. The creator is involved within the creation and shares risk and self-exposure to ambiguities and 'failures'. The creation communicates with the creator with groans beyond words, and even the elements worship their creator.

Persons encountered and remembered

As you read this, imagine you are in a nursing home for people with severe dementia. Notice your own thoughts and feelings when I tell you that in today's diary it says that the chaplain is coming to lead a service of celebration for summertime. Some staff and relatives are gathered together in the lounge with most of the residents. In the middle of the room, a table is being prepared with a brightly coloured cloth, a large candle and a bunch of flowers. Some of these flowers have been freshly cut from the garden outside with the help of some of the residents. Now music is being played, words spoken, hands gently touched with invitations to look at, take hold of, and smell the flowers. All this is followed by food and drink, including strawberries and cream! By now you may have a picture of an event where all the senses are being employed – sight, sound, touch, taste and smell. During the course of this celebration, the celebrant with his/her 'altar' introduces a classic rose – bright in colour, strong in scent yet both delicate and prickly to touch. Everyone has an opportunity to get close to it as it is brought around the room, and there is a rich variety of reactions. One of the most impaired or disabled people in the room surprises all the observers to this event. His eyes open at the scent, and on seeing the flower he names the rose. Staff are surprised and delighted by his response, which is a tangible reminder that here is an individual with both needs and abilities despite his profound disabilities. His wife recalls later that this was the last word he spoke and how each time she gave birth to their children he brought her roses. This account affirms that we are so much more than our cognitive functioning, and in providing care it is good to recognize the role of all the senses, and perhaps that special sixth sense of the transcendent or the numinous – that is, a spiritual dimension.

I met Gordon one day in the nursing home while he helped his wife, Janet, with her lunch. The husband says that he is there because he loves his wife and, having coped with her dementia for too many years on his own, wants to be with her in the extreme stages of her illness while she is cared for by others. The relatives of another resident who has died recently join us briefly and express the hope that his wife will soon be better. The husband replies that this is not possible. This was a false hope for Gordon, but a necessary hope for the visitors, so no comment was offered at the time. Later, the recently bereaved relatives talk about how death can bring necessary healing both to those who have died and the bereaved.

Teilhard de Chardin sees death not so much as the ultimate moment at which to be found receiving the sacrament of Holy Communion but rather as itself the ultimate act of Holy Communion.[10]

Ellen, at the threshold of the severe stages of dementia, was a lifelong practising Roman Catholic with a past and future but where meaning has been found in the encounter in the present moment. While living her final years in a nursing home, the chaplain (Audrey Ball), a Roman Catholic eucharistic minister, used to walk in the grounds with her as well as sit and talk and pray before sharing the sacrament. Audrey tells the story:

One lady I've been visiting regularly now for over a year, and for quite a long time I was able to give her Holy Communion. And when she became more distressed and disturbed, it wasn't always possible. But we always prayed. I would say 'Shall we pray now?' and she would always say the same thing: 'That's the best.' But one day it was different. We went for our usual walk and when we came to sit down and say, 'Shall we pray now?', before I could even start a prayer, she had started one of her own:

> Dear God
> You are all that matters
> Help us to be happy
> Help us to be welcoming
> We need each other.

I've had to learn not to become frustrated and not to judge what might be going on between one person and another in prayer. Something very special to me is the sacrament of the present moment. A person with dementia lives in the present moment.[11]

Words show something beyond themselves; we need to reflect on more than just the text to understand what is being said, in a way similar to Anton Boisen's concept of 'living human documents'.[12] Perhaps if we regard persons as living documents we need to read between the lines to reach the meaning and thereby develop what we might call an interlinear interpretation of, or approach to understanding, their personhood.

So we could offer an interpretation of the prayer offered by the lady in the midst of her experience of dementia. We could say that she addresses the Other, the ground of our Being, the 'I am that I am', about the importance of our shared moods and feelings as well as recognizing our essential interdependence. Such an insight comes out of the furnace of her experience of increasing diminishment and articulates the divinization of her passivities.[13]

Members of Christian churches share responsibility for the churches' mission to sustain people with mental as well as physical infirmities and those caring for them. The last decade or so has seen several pieces of work in the UK dedicated to responding to these needs, for example the Christian Council on Ageing's Dementia Group, Methodist Homes, Faith in the Elderly, Leeds, and more recently the Leveson Centre.[14] Although the major tasks involved are person-centred and practical ones, it is important to cultivate and promote a theology of dementia that can underpin pastoral work. Otherwise the thinking of even the best intentioned caregiver is liable to be affected by nihilistic perspectives on dementia current in modern society. An example of such a theology is to be found in orthodox theology of the Trinity.

The divine economy of the Holy Trinity, that is the perfect relationship existing between God as Father, Son and Holy Spirit, is the icon of perfect loving and community. It was this understanding which inspired Basil the Great in the fourth century to found one of the first hospitals in Caesarea where he was bishop. It grew in significance so much that a new town grew up with it at the centre. As well as founding the Eastern monastic tradition, he was one of the great teachers in early Christendom. The Cappadocian Fathers were used to both political and theological dispute as, among other topics, the early Church sought to understand and explain the person of Christ in relation to the Godhead. However, it is important to note that this was not an abstract theoretical notion in the pejorative sense that the term 'theology' is often used today in political debate. This is, rather, an example of practical theology founded upon the ethic of relatedness as both God-given and personally fulfilling. In his research on ageing in the early Christian Church, Rob Merchant has drawn attention to the considerable emphasis on social welfare reflected in the sermons, writings and actions of church leaders such as Basil and John Chrysostom. Their commitment to vulnerable older people was evident in the design of homes for the aged whose direction was a major responsibility of the local bishop.[15]

However, an examination of current advertisements in the ecclesiastical press of clerical vacancies shows that parishes' main concern is to find those clergy skilled and interested in working with young people and families; any mention of older people and people with disabilities is quite exceptional. Does the contemporary Church fail to recognize the significance of this rich and demanding area of ministry through lack of theological conviction?

This brief exploration of pastoral theology and dementia emphasizes the mysteries and paradoxes of being(s) created in the image of God. It raises the question whether dementia provides us with an image of what we all are before God, and values passivity as well as activity as persons in community and creation.

A person with dementia has the same human rights as any other citizen, and this includes access to the best quality palliative care available. Christians and all people of goodwill are challenged to give full value to the personhood of anyone with dementia and of all those involved in their care.

Justice for people with dementia is not a cheap option either in terms of personal commitment or political will. Considerably more resources will be needed in order that they may be treated as full members of society.

Notes

1   I am indebted to Gordon Bowman, Newcastle upon Tyne, for his generosity in giving me permission to use his and Janet's story here.

2   For example, *My Journey into Alzheimer's Disease*, Davies, R., Tyndale House, 1989.

3   Killick, J., *You are Words*, Hawker Publications, 1997 and *Openings: Dementia Poems and Photographs* with Cordonnier, C., Hawker Publications, 2000.

4   Kitwood, T., *Dementia Reconsidered*, Open University Press, 1997.

5   Buber, M., *I and Thou*, second edition, T & T Clark, 1958, p. 11.

6   Gibson, F., 'Can We Risk Person-Centred Communication?', *Journal of Dementia Care*, 7 (5), pp. 20–4, 1999.

7   Shamy, E. (ed.), *A Guide to the Spiritual Dimension of Care for People with Alzheimer's Disease and Related Dementia*, J. Kingsley, 2003.

8   Rose, S., *The Making of Memory: From Molecules to Mind*, Bantam Books, 1993.

9   Nicholson, T., *Black Daisies for a Bride*, TV broadcast, 1993 and published by Faber & Faber, 1994.

10 Chardin, T. d. *Le Milieu Divin*, Collins, 1960.

11 Christian Council on Ageing video, *Is Anyone There?*, 1997.

12 Foskett, J., 'Christianity and Psychiatry' in D Bhugra (ed.), *Psychiatry and Religion*, Routledge, 1996, p. 58.

13 Chardin, 1960, (op. cit.) and see Vanstone, W. H., *The Stature of Waiting*, Darton, Longman and Todd, 2004.

14 See www.leveson.org.uk for links to publications and resources from these and other sources.

15 Merchant, R., 'Ageing in the Early Church' in *Pioneering the Third Age: The Church in an Ageing Population*, Paternoster Press, 2003, pp. 99–124.

Chapter 3

A Relative's Perspective

JUDITH ALLFORD

Listening to the narrative of other lived lives is at the heart of the pastoral task. In this open, reflective story, a daughter tells the moving, ordinary and powerful story of her mother and the struggle with dementia. As you read it, try to imagine yourself in her place either as one who watches or (more problematically perhaps?) as the one with dementia. Our ability to understand and respond with compassion depends in part upon these intentional acts of imagination.

Sometimes I think I would like to write a book about living with Mum's dementia, and her dignity, faith and courage in making her tough journey to its triumphant conclusion – called something like *The Names the Good Lord Gave Us*. In the early stages, Mum began to muddle family names. She would call me by the name of her elder sister, May, who had died only recently. One day in exasperation, Mum said 'I wish we would all use the names that the good Lord gave us!' At the time we all laughed together, including Mum.

Later on, we came to see that moment as one of the signs of the way in which Mum's illness was robbing her of even the ability to recognize those closest to her. Sometimes when I was at home with her, and perhaps enjoying the sad but real privilege of providing care for her, she would not know who I was at all. But she seemed to sense I was someone she trusted, which mattered to me greatly. It mattered more that, for most of her illness, she seemed to recognize my father. One day Dad walked into the nursing home, and I said to Mum, 'Oh look, who is this come to see you?' She looked up at Dad, her husband of over 50 years, and with a wonderful smile of welcome said, 'It's the one I love.' I am sure that memory is among my father's treasures – it is certainly among mine.

It was at the turn of the millennium that I began to wonder if there was something amiss with Mum. We spoke on the phone to wish each other a Happy New Year. Mum dissolved into tears, something that she almost never did. She had to hand the phone over to Dad, who tried to reassure me by saying she was a 'little bit low'. Looking back, that was probably when the ravages of early dementia began to make themselves apparent.

At first Dad would deny that anything was wrong. In my ministry, that is something I have recognized many times. There are things too painful to see – I am sure Dad could not bear to notice the beginnings of Mum's memory loss. For several months I struggled to communicate my anxiety to Dad, and even to my brother and sister. It is true that in those early days Mum could successfully hide any sign of her illness from those whom she saw less often. The odd blips would only be apparent to those who saw her most. I remember the terror I felt when Mum explained to me that her tiredness was because she and Dad had been to stay 'up north' and the long journey had taken it out of her. I knew she had not left the bungalow for several days. It was probably around then that I first tried to enlist the help of our local church. Mum and Dad had been members for many years. Mum had run the infant Sunday School for a long time, and had only just given up leading the Women's Fellowship. For the last 25 years they had hosted a house group in their home.

I telephoned the rector, trying to be careful because I knew that Dad did not want our concerns widely known. Perhaps I was too careful. I felt I was not understood, and received only vague promises about 'keeping an eye' on my parents. However, he also said that in a large congregation there were relatively few older people needing the support of younger members. This would mean they would be able to give support when needed. The rector must at that point have enlisted the support of some of the 40- and 50-year-olds in the congregation. Two or three of them began to visit Mum and Dad regularly. The regularity in itself was important. For both Mum and Dad it lent some structure to the week. For my sister, brother and me, living away, it meant we knew when we could rely on others to be there.

Gradually it became clear that we would need medical help. Mum and Dad's GP suggested this might be the onset of Parkinson's disease and sent her for the appropriate tests. Her eyesight was clearly fading, but surgery failed to help. Mum had always been an avid reader and letter-writer, but now she began to put down her books and pen, something hugely distressing for her. She became increasingly unsteady, and fearful of walking even short distances. At first this seemed due to eyesight problems, but we began to realize she was losing her spatial awareness, and had little sense of where objects were in relation to each other. That made getting around the tiny bungalow more and more difficult. She needed a wheelchair for even the shortest journey, and was terrified of going anywhere that appeared unfamiliar. Mum began not to recognize her own home. She and Dad had lived in their bungalow for about five years, having made the decision to move from their previous house while still young and fit enough. It was Mum who had chosen the bungalow, liking both its size and location. But she couldn't remember the move, and felt that her real home was elsewhere.

In those early days she seemed bewildered, fragile, uncertain. Now I look back and wonder how it really was for her. I think that then she still had the capacity to look ahead and think about what might be in store. And yet I didn't feel able to discuss it with her – one of the things that brings me most pain. I do think that some spiritual and pastoral care from outside the family, which might have enabled Mum to explore what she was going through, might have helped. But none was forthcoming, and even I, too close to the situation, did not know what to ask for, or how.

Mum's sense of being away from home continued to deepen. Dad would take her out for a ride in the car, and when they returned, Mum would seem calmer, apparently accepting that she was back where she belonged. But one afternoon I was visiting when Dad had gone out and Mum began to ask me, with increasing anxiety, to take her home. I went to get my car keys and she asked me if I was really willing to take her home – or if I was simply going to take her out briefly, persuading her then she had indeed come home. She knew she was being deceived. I realized Mum still retained a sense of how we were trying to meet her needs – and she knew we couldn't. That too was a heartbreaking moment.

By this stage a diagnosis had been made. Mum had seen the kindly consultant at their local hospital. I attended most appointments, and I was touched to see the kindness with which Mum was treated. The consultant spoke directly to her, asking her how she felt. Mum could only say, 'I just don't feel like me.' Various tests and a CT scan followed, and Mum was referred to the elderly care consultant at the psychiatric hospital. Again, she was treated with great kindness, but the diagnosis was cruel – vascular dementia. The blood supply to her brain was slowly beginning to close down.

It was at this point that I rang the rector again to tell him that we now knew what was wrong with Mum. Unfortunately, his comment was one of the most unhelpful things said to me throughout the whole progress of Mum's illness: 'Oh well, at least now you know what you're up against, and you'll be able to make plans for her care.' Believe me, you do not know what you are up against. No one is really able to tell you how quickly, or in what way, the illness will progress. Nobody can predict what care will be needed, or when. And, even if they could, how could we begin to talk about the future, about nursing home care, or other options, to two loving, intelligent, sensitive parents who had cared for their family all their lives, and who now needed support that met the situation as it was, and as it developed, not as it might be in the future?

The next few months saw Mum's mental state continue to deteriorate. The greatest support at this time came from the Community Psychiatric Nurse who had been assigned to Mum. Both Mum and Dad took to Anthea and trusted her. She visited regularly and would sit patiently discussing with Mum the way in which her mind was 'playing tricks' on her. Many times we thanked God for Anthea.

I can only pay the very highest tribute to the way in which both Mum and Dad continued to face her illness. Dad's care for her was heartbreakingly complete. And Mum, even in her confusion and fear, remained her lovely, gentle self. Early in 2002 she and Dad celebrated their 50th Wedding Anniversary. Obviously it would not have been possible to have a party for them. So my siblings and I wrote to some of the very many friends that Mum and Dad had treasured through the years and asked if they would be kind enough simply to send greetings and a photo, so that Mum and Dad could remember together. The response was wonderful. All through Mum's illness it remained an incredible privilege to see how she fought to hold on to her sense of self and her appreciation of others. Her essential goodness never deserted her.

Mum's mobility had almost gone and she could not get around the bungalow without help. She seemed to have forgotten how to walk. Tragic though that seemed at the time, later we were to count it a blessing. But it meant that Dad was caring for her, with the assistance of carers, right round the clock. One particular afternoon, Mum's mobility suddenly, briefly, returned. Somehow she found her way to the kitchen where she fell, and fractured her neck of femur. Poignantly, Dad now acknowledges that when the ambulance drove away, he felt a sense of relief – relief that someone else would now take responsibility for Mum's care.

At first it seemed likely that Mum was too fragile to come through surgery on her hip. But, remarkably, she survived surgery and the first few days of trauma care. It was as she began to recover physically that the dementia became ever more apparent. So too did the demands that her needs placed on already fraught staff. All her life, Mum had wanted to give no trouble. Had her mind been clear, she would have asked for help only as a last resort. Now she could not ask for help, even when she most needed it. Staff found it hard to appreciate that Mum simply did not understand how to use the 'buzzer' to call for assistance. Mum's needs, and her limited understanding, must have been terribly frustrating for staff, but we know that they sometimes spoke 'sharply' to her, and this felt deeply unacceptable. One or two of the ward team took time to get to know Mum, and, in doing so, grew to love her. We knew that we could rely on their kindness, and it was always reassuring to find one of them on duty.

It was also hard for staff to appreciate that, as a family, we were still struggling to come to terms with Mum's vascular dementia. Those caring for her now had not known Mum previously, and accepted what they saw as the 'norm'. For us it was very far from the norm. In the midst of an environment which seemed at times insensitive and uncaring, all of us, and most especially Mum, were wrestling with frightening new evidence of the disease process. Looking back now, I do believe Mum was frightened for very much of the time. Not all the time, because we know that our favourite health care assistant, Amanda, was able sometimes to draw her out of herself and laugh and joke with her. But for much of the time, Mum was probably terrified – as so many of the dementia patients in our acute hospital wards must be. Ironically, if Mum's accident had happened only a few weeks earlier, she would have been transferred eventually to a ward specializing in the care of the elderly mentally infirm, a ward which had a good reputation for its high standards of care. But cutbacks had forced the ward to close just before Mum's admission.

By now we were becoming aware of another process of transition within Mum. When I later had the privilege of conducting her funeral service, I drew special attention to it. In his second letter to the Corinthians, the apostle Paul wrote that 'though outwardly we are wasting away, yet inwardly we are being renewed day by day'. Mum was wasting away physically, and mentally even more so. But increasingly we saw that the inner core of her being remained strong. Mum's spirituality and belief had always been very private to her, typical of her generation and character. But we had always known that her faith was very real, and, as their children, are indebted to both our parents for their example of Christian living. But now Mum's relationship with God was becoming ever more apparent. On one occasion, while Mum was in bed, and obviously in some discomfort, I suggested we might sing the words of her favourite hymn, 'In Heavenly Love Abiding'. Mum seemed so weak and frail until she began to sing – and with her soft, true voice she sang with me every verse of that hymn, leading me in the words when I stumbled. She had forgotten so much, but not the things that mattered to her most.

Mum had left school at fourteen, but in a later generation would have gone to university, as her children all did. She was very bright, not least with words, and it was hard to see her vocabulary increasingly deserting her. Yet almost to the end of her life, there were times when she would astonish us with the accuracy and complexity of a word or phrase. One of those times was in hospital, when she suddenly said to my father, 'Majestically Alive.' Dad asked her to repeat and she did, very firmly and with a smile. She couldn't explain it, but it obviously brought her a rare joy, and, even then, I understood that she was starting to look beyond what we could see.

On another occasion I said 'Goodbye' to her. She looked at me, and said, very clearly: 'The Lord watch between thee and me whilst we are parted.' I had never heard her say that before and I went home to look it up. I found it in Genesis 31.49, where Laban departs from Jacob. We had always sensed that Mum found partings from her children very hard. Maybe she had always used that as a prayer for us. Had it not been for her illness, we should never have known that. I took care to use it as often as I could when saying 'Goodbye' to her after that, and we printed it on the cover of her funeral service.

It was becoming increasingly obvious that Mum would not be able to return home. We as a family, and especially my father, had to get used to the idea. We had not expected Mum to survive surgery – in some ways it would have seemed a mercy if she had not. But she did, and physically she was recovering very well, seemingly against the odds. A multi-disciplinary team meeting was arranged to discuss alternative care. The meeting proposed nursing home care and, as a family, we set about looking for somewhere right for Mum. But our search was not without heartache. Dad felt a deep sense of failure, and I considered the possibility of giving up my job, at least for a while. My manager asked how I could possibly know what length of time commitment I would be making. And of course I couldn't know. My mind returned to the glib comment about being able to make plans for Mum's care. How can you plan when the future seems fragile and unknown?

A miracle happened. Within days Dad had heard that a room in a suitable home had become available, and we were invited to go and look at it. I prayed that there would be a clear sign of God's hand. On a beautiful August day in 2002 we were shown into a room on the first floor. Sunlight was streaming through the windows. The windows – plural! The receptionist who was showing us round told us very cheerfully that this was one of the very few rooms with two windows. I never fail to thank God for that room. We accepted it for Mum. We had a few brief days to make Mum's room her own. Dad got friends to move in her bureau, where Mum had done so much of her writing through the years. We sorted her clothes and prepared a wardrobe for her. It was hard to know whether to feel sad or relieved. At last she would be out of hospital, but it seemed unlikely that she would ever return to the bungalow. We all continued to wrestle with the way we felt about what was happening. People sometimes say that they would not want to put their loved one 'away' in a home. Now we were thinking of doing that with Mum. But I recalled how I had tried to help others facing this situation. I had tried to encourage them that they would be able to treasure and enjoy the time they spent with their relative. Now I had to believe that for myself. I understood the logic, but I still struggled with it. We talked round and round the situation as a family. My brother, who is younger than my sister and me, had spent a lot of time alone with Mum when he was growing up and we had already left home. She had shared with him things we did not know. She had once told him that, if she grew infirm in old age, we were 'not to worry' if we felt she needed nursing home care. With the selflessness she always showed to us, Mum had told David she wanted us to lead our own lives and that we were not to be burdened by her care.

Mum's move to her new home went as smoothly as any discharge from an acute hospital. Transport was delayed and my father was glad that he had stayed to travel with her. I met them when they arrived. Mum was exhausted. The sister suggested that Dad and I had a cup of tea while they put Mum to bed. I can still picture Mum asleep in bed at the end of that afternoon. She looked comfortable for the first time since she had gone to hospital. Because she was so unable to help herself, she could never sit comfortably in a chair without sliding forward, and she was unable to move around in bed. Now, at least for the time being, she seemed relaxed and at peace. I wish that I could say that things were perfect after that. Of course they were not, but they were as good as it gets under the circumstances, and very much better than the experience of many people. Staff at the nursing home seemed to show kindness to Mum, and gradually learned to accept and understand her limitations.

When we first met the matron of the home, she told us that as a family it would take us longer to settle in than it did Mum, and she was proved right. In our minds, I suppose, nobody could ever care for Mum the way that we wished we could have done. My father, bereaved of my mother's presence in their home after over 50 years of marriage, grieved very much that things had to be this way. Throughout the two-and-a-half years which followed, Dad visited Mum every day. He, like all of us as a family, was constantly alert to any sign of poor standards in Mum's care. We found mercifully few such signs, and constant indications that, in fact, her care was very good indeed.

It was hard to tell whether or not Mum was happy, but we always felt that we would have known had she been significantly *un*happy. Mum had been naturally a very shy person, and may well have appreciated the fact that little interaction with the other residents was possible, because many of them were also cognitively impaired to some degree. Sometimes I wondered if she was lonely because she spent a lot of time alone. But much of that time she spent sleeping. I used to wonder a lot how things were for her at night. Did she wake up not knowing where she was? Was she ever afraid at night? Did the staff call in to check that she was all right and not restless? Gradually we began to realize that the staff were becoming more familiar with Mum's needs than we were. Just as importantly, they were clearly growing to love Mum. Beneath her confusion and disorientation, Mum continued to remain the person she had always been. She never failed to show appreciation for her care, repeatedly thanking the staff for everything they did for her, great or small. She tried to help them as much as she could. And when she felt well enough, she would treat them to her wonderful smile. Even her sense of humour was sometimes apparent in those early days.

One of our great hopes had been that Mum's friends from church would continue to visit her in the nursing home. I think perhaps at first some of them did come to see her. But the visitors soon dropped away. I found this desperately hard. Mum had always been tireless in her interest in others and her care for them. She and Dad had done a lot of visiting elderly and frail friends over the years. I suppose I felt resentful that the same love and care was not being afforded to her in return. But we soon fell into a pattern, and I was able to visit Mum most weeks. Very often, Margaret, my close friend, came with me. I don't know if I could have managed without her support. Margaret had always been very fond of Mum, and she was able to view our situation with a greater objectivity than I could and brought a much needed sense of balance. My sister, Elizabeth, and my brother David, shared the visiting. Mum showed the greatest pleasure when Elizabeth brought her three boys to see Nanna. For much of the time she could still converse with them, and always asked them about themselves, just as she had done when she was well.

In a sense I could appreciate why friends found it hard to be with Mum. Many of them had known her for many years. When they visited now, she sometimes didn't seem to know who they were. Conversation was difficult, and she would almost certainly not be able to remember their visit after they had gone. It must have been easy to think that their visits didn't matter, or that they made no difference. I still think that is a pity, because I believe that even a brief visit did matter very much at the time. Many times I had a sense that it was important to Mum that someone was there. Being with her was about seizing the moment, and some days there were very good moments. I remember when I was struggling to help her back onto the bed from her chair, I was getting into a terrible muddle, and suddenly realized that Mum was doubled up with laughter at my antics. That was very special.

Looking back, I understand more clearly now that the leaders of my parents' home church probably felt that they were discharging their duty of pastoral care to Mum and Dad through other members of the congregation. Liz was visiting Mum regularly, and Dad was also being visited each week by one or two of the church members who had begun calling on them when Mum was still living in their bungalow. As a family we were very grateful for their care. At the same time another member of the lay pastoral team was making occasional visits to Mum. Sadly, however, she was not someone whom Mum had known well, and we were realizing more and more the value of the familiar. We treasured the occasional visits of Hazel, a missionary friend of my parents, who would call in when she was home on furlough. Hazel is a nurse, and was always comfortable with Mum. I cannot be sure if the rector of the Church visited Mum at all while she was in the nursing home, but he may have done so once or twice. I know that the deacon did visit – perhaps once every couple of months. Neither of them visited Dad at home during that time, as far as I am aware. My sister, brother and I were torn through by anguish not only for Mum, who, as time went on, was probably less aware of her circumstances, and our sorrow for Dad, whose loneliness and grief must have been unbearable at times. Both were of the generation where they would have hidden their feelings, wherever possible, and I am sure that it would not have occurred to Dad to ask for spiritual or pastoral support for himself.

I think Mum would have benefited a great deal from the regular receiving of Holy Communion, or a very simple ministry of prayer. Dad felt that the ministry of the sacrament would be less important to Mum than perhaps it was to us. Mum had grown up in the Methodist Church and had not been accustomed to receiving Holy Communion each week. In one sense, I think Dad had a very valid point. We were beginning to see that Mum was finding refuge more and more in the past. In Mum's young days her faith had been very active, but probably not often expressed by the formal receiving of Communion. Perhaps the familiarity of the administration to her was more in my mind than it would have been in hers. However, I do think that Mum would have firmly believed that the sacrament of Holy Communion is indeed 'an outward and visible sign of an inward and spiritual grace' and I believe that she would have been nourished and blessed accordingly. I felt frustrated and angry that the same thought did not seem to occur to the clergy team. However, clergy from the local parish did visit the nursing home each month, and held a service of Holy Communion in the residents' lounge. Afterwards, they would bring extended Communion to those who were not well enough to sit through the service. Mum usually went back to bed after lunch, and then stayed in her own room, where Dad visited her so faithfully. But on several occasions, at least, she received Communion with Dad. On one of those afternoons I happened to be with Mum, and was able to receive Communion with her. I was very touched by the sensitive way in which 'Revd Lucy', as she was affectionately known, both talked and prayed with Mum. It was the briefest of services, but it embraced Mum and her family by name, and it enabled Mum to join in the Lord's Prayer and to receive a Blessing.

So why didn't I put on my collar and bring Communion to my own mother, as I was doing week by week to our hospital patients, including very often those with some degree of dementia? I think there were several reasons for that. One was that I felt it would breach professional etiquette. I was not my parents' priest and I did not feel it was my place to minister the sacrament to Mum. Another was that to Mum, first and foremost, I was her daughter and not her pastor. Mum and Dad have always been hugely supportive of me in my ministry. On occasion she had heard me preach, or conduct a service. Most recently, just before she became ill, she had invited me to speak at a women's World Day of Prayer service at their church. But she would not have known me primarily as a priest. The third reason is probably the simplest and most powerful: I did not really feel I had the strength to offer that ministry to Mum. Like my sister, brother and, most of all, my father, I was so very distressed by Mum's illness. I cannot describe adequately what a good woman Mum was. I watched the ravages of this illness upon her, and sometimes I raged inwardly at the apparent injustice of it. I needed, and I felt my father needed too, someone to come to minister to us alongside Mum.

On one occasion, when Mum was in hospital, the church deacon had done just that. I was on my own with Mum, and Caroline had arrived unexpectedly. She didn't stay very long, which I appreciated, but she stayed long enough to chat with both Mum and me. And she prayed very simply with us both. I know that I was moved to tears by her kindness and apparent understanding. As she left, she touched me gently on the shoulder, told me to try not to worry, and promised that the team would care for Mum and for Dad. I suppose the staff team did feel that they fulfilled this responsibility through others. But I felt let down and disappointed. In my own ministry I have had the great privilege of being alongside senior members of the clergy, both of whom were going through an experience similar to ours. They have asked me to pray with them and with their loved one. Both told me that when they were facing the illness of someone dear to them, they needed the spiritual care of another priest. One of them, a newly consecrated bishop, said that, to his own mother, he needed first to be son.

That has helped me to know that I am not alone. If I am honest, I think that, as an ordained priest, I have felt let down by my own colleagues – let down both for myself, and on behalf of my family. At the same time, it has brought home to me something of the significance of the very many occasions on which those to whom I have sought to minister must have felt let down by me. All of us know that we cannot do everything, and nor can we be constantly haunted by the things we have failed to do. We try endlessly to prioritize, and perhaps comfort ourselves, rightly, with the knowledge that Jesus himself left unmet need. But I know also that the phone call I failed to make may well have left its mark of hurt and disappointment. I, too, need to be forgiven.

But those who did not visit Mum missed a blessing. Over those many months in the nursing home, I believe we truly saw the radiance of the Lord Jesus within her, and I believe that others saw and recognized it too. I shall never forget one of the nursing sisters who spoke to me the day after Mum died, and said that she believed the angels would have taken Mum 'straight home' because she had been an angel herself – and that was where she belonged. That sister was talking about someone who had become so fractured in mind that she had even been unable to learn the names of those who cared for her so tenderly. But in her spirit she had continued to be restored day by day.

Music had always been part of Mum's life. Methodism was born in song! Dad is a pianist, and through the years would often play for us the old hymns that meant so much to her. As children we learned to love much of the music that she knew, and the words that went with them. In the nursing home we could continue to share that love with Mum. Like Liz, we would often pick up Mum's hymnbook and read, or even sing to her, the words of familiar hymns. So very often, Mum would join in with us, even on the days when she seemed least aware of her surroundings, or of our presence. When I sang with her, she could still, as she always had, hold the note far better than I could! We had also, incidentally, been delighted to find some of the music of the Cliff Adams Singers on tape. For most of my childhood we had not had a television, and the 'wireless' featured large in our lives. We listened to *Sing Something Simple* together, and now we were able to do that again with Mum. I had previously had only a very limited understanding of the value both of music and reminiscence in the care of a patient who is both elderly and confused, and we proved that value now. We played the tapes softly always – and hoped the nurses did the same. Mum had always been a very quiet person, and very early on in her illness we learned that noise and bustle could agitate her further. But we hoped that, in the gentleness of the music, there was peace.

For many years Mum had led the Women's Fellowship at the church. She had done so faithfully and conscientiously week by week, and we knew that she had been well loved there. But we had little idea of her ministry to that group of elderly women, some of whom had little else in terms of regular links with the Church. In Mum's days in the nursing home we and the staff surprisingly found ourselves learning something about those meetings. Mum would sit in the residents' lounge morning by morning, with the other elderly residents, mostly women, gathered there also. Sometimes, it seemed Mum would perceive herself to be back in the position of leading the weekly meeting. The staff would notice that she would begin to suggest hymns, to invite the congregation, as she saw it to be, to share in prayer, and sometimes she would even lead in the Lord's Prayer. We don't imagine that the others joined in – most of them would have been unable to do so – but the staff noticed, and questioned us about it.

One day, when I was enjoying Mum's company in her room, a similar thing happened. For a few moments Mum was back in the meeting room at the church, encouraging the women in her care as she led in prayer for the needs of the world and of those around them. It was a breathtaking privilege. So self-effacing had Mum been that we would never have known about the firm and gentle way in which she clearly led her congregation, had her illness not brought it to us like this. In so very many ways we learned more about Mum, and about her great love for Jesus, through her illness, than we had ever known before. In the strangest of ways, I found I was beginning to thank God for something I had so feared.

In a remarkable way, too, Mum continued to witness to those around her of the love of the Lord Jesus and of the steadfastness of her faith in him. We had been warned that the illness and disorientation could cause Mum to become aggressive, and there were occasional moments when we saw this. But never to anything like the extent we had been advised could be possible, although we recognize that there would have been things the staff did not tell us. But we never heard Mum swear, or blaspheme, or deal in any way unkindly with those who were trying to help her. On only one occasion did Mum shout at me – and that was when I had gone to visit her wearing a pair of jeans. Mum didn't recognize me, very possibly because she couldn't place me in that particular attire. She shouted at me to go away, and then called the staff to 'get this ragamuffin away from me'! Distressing though it was, there was also a funny side to it, and I felt I had only myself to blame. I also was very pleased that Mum still had not lost her wide vocabulary.

But of course she continued to deteriorate day by day. The process was quite gentle in so many ways, but it seemed to us to be a process of little losses gradually, and sometimes we would become aware that those little losses, taken together, had become something far greater. I found myself wondering how I would know when Mum had spoken my name for the last time. Margaret always encouraged me to live for the moment – something I find very hard under any circumstances. But it was such sound advice in this situation. I needed to treasure what I had, savour those moments of recognition, the times when Mum still addressed me by the pet name she had used for my sister and me for all the years of our lives. I needed to treasure each special moment as if it were the last, because I did not know otherwise.

I wish I could convey something of the laughter we shared as well. Mum continued to hallucinate, although the things she saw did not often seem to disturb or frighten her. But also, as she retreated into the past, she took us with her and shared the concerns of what was, for her, the moment. One example of this had to do with Mum's vocabulary. It was increasingly hard for us to fathom how Mum's mind, shutting down second by second as it seemed to us, could retain such complex and beautifully descriptive words and phrases. But sometimes Mum would introduce a word which none of us had ever heard, and which almost certainly didn't exist. I wish I could remember an actual example of this, but the one I will use is hypothetical, I'm afraid. Mum might say 'Where's the "boddon"? We would struggle to be helpful, but would have to admit that we didn't know what we were looking for. 'What did you say, Mum?'. ' I said – "Where's the boddon? – B O Double D O N BODDON!" Mum was clearly exasperated by our ignorance!

In February 2005, I had planned to take a week's annual leave. I was to spend the first two or three days with my parents and then I was going to Norway for four days. There was an answer-phone message from Sue, the sister who had first admitted Mum to the nursing home, and who knew Mum and Dad well. We learned afterwards that Sue had left a similar message for my sister, and had also tried to reach me at work. In all the time that Mum had been in the nursing home, the staff had never had cause to ring us. Despite Mum's apparent frailty and the steady march of the disease, physically she had kept very well over the last two-and-a-half years. So, as I listened to Sue's message, despite her encouragement 'not to worry', I realized when she said Mum did not seem very well that day and that the doctor had been called, that this was serious.

When we got to the home, Sue told us that they had called the doctor because they felt that Mum may have had a slight stroke, and that the doctor had been and had promised to come again on Monday. Mum was asleep when we went into her room, but it was clear from her appearance that the diagnosis of a stroke was probably an accurate one. We sat quietly with her, and I remember reflecting that this was what the psychiatric consultant had told us three years ago. Mum would effectively have constant 'mini' strokes, but eventually she would have a more major episode, and this would almost certainly be terminal. I felt so grateful to God for his timing. I had ten days ahead of me without having to worry about work, and about arranging cover if I couldn't be there. All that was already in hand. I was grateful to be there with Mum and Dad. Our family had always tried to share our support for them, as best we could. Elizabeth was there with Dad when Mum went into A & E after her fall. I was glad that I had the freedom to offer support on this occasion.

During that weekend, both Elizabeth and David came home. We knew that Mum was very poorly, and that the end could be near. We talked with Dad about what we should do if the GP recommended that Mum went into hospital. I know that Dad had very mixed feelings. On the one hand, he did not want Mum to be caused further distress by being uprooted from her familiar surroundings. On the other, he wondered if she would stand a better chance of recovery if she went into hospital. I know that my feelings were very influenced by the memory of the poor care that Mum had received on her previous admission. I also knew that an acute hospital is not the best place for an elderly demented patient.

Together, and individually, we wrestled with that dilemma all weekend. I was comforted by a conversation I had had with Mum not long after she first became ill. She had said to me that she did not expect that she would be with us for very much longer. But, she said, 'I don't want you to worry about me, because I know where I am going, and you know where I will be.' I had treasured those words, and the privilege of receiving them from Mum. I think Mum had feared what her journey might entail, but she did not fear her destination. It seemed to me that the time had come to let Mum at last go home.

I think we probably all came to the same decision, but it happened to be me who was there when the GP came on Monday. As I arrived at the home in the morning, I was greeted by one of the sisters with the news that the doctor was with Mum. I burst into tears, begging her to persuade him to let Mum stay in the care of the home. She told me that the staff had agreed that they would be very happy to care for Mum, but felt that I needed to speak to the doctor myself. The doctor was very kind and very pleasant, but he was young, and I knew that he was struggling not to get this wrong.

I could see his preoccupation with the looming shadow of litigation. Sadly, I knew only too well where he was coming from. I was also sure now that we were seeking the right thing for Mum. Eventually he gently agreed that Mum could stay in the home for a few days and then he would assess her again to see if she needed extra care. How we prayed that those days would be enough.

The following morning, the rightness of our decision was underlined in a very practical way. Had Mum gone into hospital she would have been 'nil by mouth'. I went to see her at breakfast time to find her being fed her favourite porridge! The next dilemma for me was whether to go away. Margaret and I had booked a short trip on the Hurtigruten. I love the tranquillity and beauty of Norway and I had been looking forward to going. Mum was now bedridden and sleeping for much of the time. Elizabeth, who is a teacher and classroom assistant, was now on half-term holiday and planned to spend as much time as she could with Dad. David, who is much further away in Yorkshire, would be back at the weekend.

Suddenly it seemed right to go. The staff at the home promised me they would care for Mum. They had no need to tell me that: I knew they would.

But it was with great sadness that I said 'Goodbye' to Mum. I knew that it was very unlikely that she would still be there when we got back. But I also knew that she would at last be going home. I know that Caroline, the deacon from the church, came in to see Mum at least twice during those ten days. I had met her the day before I was due to go away, as she was leaving, and I was arriving to see Mum. I am glad that she came, but I still find it difficult not to think that she had left it too late. The rector didn't come, and I remember my sister being upset because he did not ask her or Dad after the Sunday service how things were with Mum.

On the Monday, the day I was due home, Mum took a turn for the worse. I was due back that evening. Severe snow had almost delayed our journey another night, and I think ours was the last plane to take off from Oslo airport that day. During the evening, Mum's breathing became increasingly laboured, and her final struggle began. I know that Dad and Elizabeth found it very hard, but they stayed with Mum until the end. At about 10 o'clock, just as our plane was landing, God took Mum home, and for the last time Elizabeth said for her our childhood prayer.

Elizabeth stayed with Dad that night and I went to be with them the following morning. We knew that there was much to be done, but it was also very important for me to hear the account of those last days. I remain so very glad that Elizabeth was able to be with Dad and Mum.

Dad had chosen a lovely family firm of funeral directors. Terry, who made Mum's arrangements with us, could not have been more helpful, or more professional. We stumbled over who would conduct the service. Mum had never been close to the rector and, in any case, he had seen so little of her that I, at least, felt that it would be inappropriate to ask him. We had booked the service for the following Friday week, only to discover too late that Caroline was due to be away at the start of a church weekend. We contacted the former rector, whom Mum had liked and respected, but he lived some distance away, and felt too frail to travel. His compassion, however, was very real. He also promised me that he would contact Dad again after the funeral.

He kept that promise, as I knew he would, and it meant a great deal to me. Tentatively I offered to take the service for Mum. Dad, I think, had hoped for that, but was worried that I would find it 'too much'. I knew I wanted to do it. Much of the service was already planned. Dad had chosen as our opening hymn, 'For I know whom I have believed'. For me, this was an even more significant choice than Dad could have known. Throughout my anxiety about Mum, from the beginning of her illness until its end, Paul's words from 2 Timothy 1.12 on which that hymn is based, 'For I know whom I have believed, and am persuaded that he is able to keep that which I have committed unto him against that day', had brought the greatest comfort to me. I had always felt that, as we entrusted Mum to him, God would not fail to protect and take care of her. To sing this hymn at Mum's funeral service would be both a testimony to her faith and a celebration of God's faithfulness. And of course we included also, 'In heavenly love abiding'.

Many people came to say 'Farewell' to Mum, including some of those who she had worked alongside in Sunday School, or to whom she had ministered at the weekly Fellowship. All the house group members were there, as were some of the mission partners whom Mum and Dad had faithfully supported through the years. We were touched at the many kind words that were said to us of Mum, and touched by those who very clearly felt indebted to her for her kindness and example. Two acts of kindness by my own friends were especially meaningful to me. One of my colleagues at the hospital, a Roman Catholic sister, took the time out to travel down for the service. And another close friend, Di, who had never met Mum but who had always been ready with understanding and support for me, offered to come and be in my parents' bungalow while we were at the service, and cook a meal to be ready on our return. It was an offering of great thoughtfulness, and was deeply appreciated.

The rector of the church attended the service. The day after Mum had died he had called on Dad. I knew that I would find it hard to talk with him, and so I had taken the opportunity to go back to the nursing home. I know that Dad valued his visit, which mattered greatly, and also that he understood why I could not be there. I know that he must have had his own reasons for not spending more time with Mum. I think perhaps those reasons were probably very sound ones. I understand enough about life in a parish to know how very busy it can be – and how relentless in its demands. With my professional head I can understand very well. But, as Mum's daughter, I suppose that the sense that he did not value Mum enough to take time to be with her, still hurts me. Dementia is like any other illness – except that dementia attacks the brain. It is too easy to think that, at the same time, it diminishes the person who is suffering from it. It did not diminish Mum, not one bit. In fact, in the eyes of those who loved her best, and of those who spent most time with her, she grew in the stature of her spirit day by day.

During the ten days that followed Mum's death, there had been things to frustrate us and to make us smile, and I suppose to distract us a little from the greatness of our loss. The GP – not the doctor who had attended Mum in her last illness, but a senior colleague – made a mess of the completion of Mum's death certificate. She had stated 'Alzheimer's disease' as the cause of death. I felt exasperated by that. It was incorrect, and no less wrong than if she had entered 'cancer' or any other condition. She was very irritated when

I returned the certificate to her, and on the second version she recorded the date of Mum's death incorrectly. Finally we got it right, but I did not feel I was treated with any great compassion along the way, either by the doctor or by the practice staff. I felt that it was being made clear to me that it was the living, and not the dead, who deserved time and trouble to be taken.

Fortunately, I was in a world I understood. GP practice managers and Medical Death Certificates hold no fears for me. But I was glad that it was not Dad who was dealing with this, and I wondered how others might have dealt with the off-handedness extended to me. In complete contrast, the Registrar and her staff could not have been kinder, or more helpful.

In fairness, I need also to record that the GP rang Dad later that day, after her surgery, to offer her condolences to him, and also to apologize for the mistakes that had been made. That mattered a great deal to Dad.

Our smiles were on the day of Mum's funeral itself, and were reserved for the town crematorium. Only once had Dad previously attended a service at that crematorium. It was a fairly new building, and my siblings and I had not seen it before. From my seat in the front of the limousine I could see both my brother's face and Margaret's as we swung into the crematorium gates and up the long driveway. Afterwards David said that it had reminded him of an especially bad transatlantic theme park! Fortunately we all knew that Mum would have seen the funny side of it, and of the cinema organ which led us into the chapel. It was good to feel that she was smiling with us.

There was only one final act that we could perform for Mum, and that was to lay her mortal remains to rest in an appropriate way. I felt quite irrationally clear that her ashes should be removed from the crematorium as soon as possible, and the amused and sympathetic funeral directors were happy to follow our instructions. The town cemetery is close to the nursing home where Mum had spent her last years. It is beautifully kept, and surprisingly peaceful, despite being surrounded by busy roads.

So much that was so very good came out of both Mum's living and her dying. Mum's gift of friendship, which she had quietly offered to so many through the years, continued to bless us now that she was gone. It was wonderful to be able to talk to Auntie June in Perth, Western Australia, with whom Mum had corresponded since they were both seventeen years old. They had met less than half a dozen times, but their friendship had been invaluable to them both, and we knew that Auntie June mourned Mum's passing very greatly. Yet, across the miles, she comforted us. So too did other friends, not so far away, but of equally long standing.

We can never bear adequate testimony to God's goodness to us all. After Mum had died, and I made a visit to the nursing home, I made a remarkable discovery. The new matron, who had indeed come into post just as

Mum had suffered her final stroke, had, of course, a nursing background. But that background was a specialist background – in palliative care. She was only to stay in post at the home for a few brief months, but she was there all through Mum's final week, advising and supporting the nurses and carers as they looked after Mum. Her qualifications had been the main reason why we heard no more about the need for Mum to go into hospital. We, and most of all Mum, had been provided for in every detail.

One other promise of God which I so treasured on the way is Psalm 37.25 – 'I was young and now I am old, yet I have never seen the righteous forsaken': how true that was. And Mum had always prided herself on the fact that, like her mother before her, her hair had not grown grey in old age. Towards the very end of her life, it grew a little grey. But God had said – 'Even to your old age and grey hairs I am he, I am he who will sustain you' (Isaiah 46.4). Looking back over what I have written, I hope I have not painted a rosier picture than it was. Especially for Mum's sake, I would not want to minimize her suffering, or what must have been her fear. But both her suffering, and ours, was very different from the suffering which must come from watching a loved one die in terrible pain. Perhaps Mum's was a gentler road than that.

And I am aware too of how very blessed we were. Blessed in a way which perhaps others facing similar situations would feel not themselves to be. Maybe we had choices available to us which others do not have. There were relatively few occasions when we felt, on behalf of Mum, that we had been let down by the systems which should have been in place to help us. For others, that experience is sadly very much more commonplace. We marvelled, and we continue to marvel, at the care that we and Mum received.

Perhaps too we had only limited experience of the misunderstanding and stigma which can attach itself so easily to the illnesses of the mind. I have recorded what was at times only a sense of neglect on the part of those I felt should have known better. Others coping with dementia for themselves or for a loved one carry burdens that are infinitely greater than that.

For Mum's funeral service, my sister made a wonderful collage of photos of Mum, a vivid reminder of all that she is to us all. So many of those photos are bright with Mum's smile. She almost never lost her smile, and, in her journey through the wilderness of bewilderment, she showed us that, to walk in the way of the cross is to find it none other than the way of life and peace. She died in Lent 2005, and Easter came for her before it did for us! I close with the words of our childhood prayer: 'Lord, keep us safe this night, secure from all our fears. May angels guard us while we sleep, 'til morning light appears. Amen.' Amen.

SECTION 2

Quality of Life for People with Dementia

Chapter 4

Communication, Faith and People with Dementia

MARGARET ANNE TIBBS

There are many examples of innovative work among people living with dementia. A number of centres (particularly the Bradford Dementia Group) have been established to co-ordinate research in order to improve the quality of care. In this technical but accessible piece, Margaret Anne Tibbs, a social worker and trainer, takes us through the process of a research study at Methodist Homes that highlights a number of significant elements for good care. Here she considers the important issue of communication with people with dementia and explores ways in which faith survives or fails to survive under this assault on the self. The reader is given access to some of the key writings in dementia care and the chapter allows the voice of older people to be heard.

Introduction: 'Who is it that can tell me who I am?'

This quotation from *King Lear* by Shakespeare was used by Archbishop Rowan Williams in a televised interview – and when I heard the question asked in this form, I realized that it encapsulated what I hope to say in this chapter.

I shall be attempting to explore areas of identity and spirituality in the light of my experiences in the research project 'A New Picture of Care' on which I worked from 1998 to 2001.

Shakespeare, writing nearly 400 years ago, was clearly familiar with dementia. He puts the following words into the mouth of Lear (Act 4, Scene 7):

I am a very foolish fond old man, Fourscore and upward, not an hour more nor less; And, to deal plainly, I fear I am not in my perfect mind. Methinks I should know you, and know this man; Yet I am doubtful . . .

Shakespeare is describing what we now, subscribing to the prevailing medical discourse of dementia, describe as the disease process of dementia. In his day, such mental decline appears to be associated with the fact that Lear is very old.

So, if I have dementia and ask, 'Who is it that can tell me who I am?' (Act 1, Scene 4), the answer has to be: those who are looking after me. Those who will stand with me, who will care for me through my problems in communicating, through my frustrations, my episodes of agonizing awareness of what I have lost, my rages and my tears, the times when I withdraw within my own head in protest at the unforgiving world in which I find myself.

Our sense of our own identity is one of the aspects of our humanity which is seriously undermined by dementia. This is because it depends on memory, which is one of the early casualties of the neurological damage. We need to be able to remember our own story and the story of the significant people in our lives. It is these stories which tell us who we are. Without memory and a sense of who we are, we are living in a place which undermines our very humanity.

As Lear says (Act 2, Scene 4):

> . . . we are not ourselves
> When nature, being oppressed, commands the mind
> To suffer with the body.

If we can no longer remember our own story, we are dependent upon other people to hold on to it for us. This depends on other people caring enough about us and having enough time and skill to tell our own story back to us. What are our chances of us finding such people?

Our sense of our identity is strongly linked to our ability to communicate with language. Sadly, this is also eroded by dementia. As the precise and accurate words we use to convey what we mean are lost, we start to rely more on metaphor and poetic imagery. Later still, we resort more and more to non-verbal communication, and eventually our primary means of communication is our behaviour – actions speak louder than words. Just as we depend on other people to hold our identity for us, we also depend upon others to have enough time and to be sufficiently motivated to decode our fractured and fragmented language. We depend on others to decipher our code.

There is a Zulu proverb which means, 'A person becomes a person through other people' – 'Umuntu ukumuntu ngybanye abantu'. In other words, we only develop and maintain our status as human beings through relationships with other human beings. If we develop dementia, we are in grave danger of becoming non-persons – partly because the fading sense of who we are becomes increasingly difficult to communicate to other people. We can reach a place where we are totally dependent upon other people taking the time and trouble to find out how to sustain our well-being. We are no longer able to sustain it for ourselves.

If we are honest, we have to admit that many people do not find it easy to engage with people with dementia at any level other than the most superficial. This applies to many family members as well as those who care for them in a professional capacity.

People who are very disturbed and tormented, whose behaviour is chaotic and apparently meaningless, frighten us. This apparent meaninglessness is very disturbing. Those who fail to respond to us are equally disturbing to most people. The lack of any interaction – the absence of clear evidence whether the person is awake or asleep – is hard to handle. 'Is there any point?' we ask ourselves.

These deep anxieties collude with the prevailing shortage of the resources of money and staff in care homes to condone our failure to engage with people with dementia on a personal level. This collusion gives respectability to our neglect. It makes it seem all right to ignore these fellow human beings on the grounds that 'they are in a world of their own' and to say that 'they don't know what's happening to them – therefore it doesn't really matter if we ignore them'.

Since the research project finished, I have been working as a trainer. In the past two years I have worked with care staff from many different settings in many different places, providing training in person-centred care. In every training session I meet some individuals who are not only willing but anxious to learn new caring techniques and who express a powerful desire to 'make a difference' to people's lives. They are aware that they do not know enough. They are looking for answers, reasons, wanting to understand puzzling behaviour, looking for new ways to try and help. These people often feel very validated when they are given a narrative which fits their own experience.

The narrative of person-centred dementia care was first written down by Tom Kitwood in the early 1990s. He developed it from his work as a Rogerian psychologist with other client groups. Of course, many people were already providing person-centred care, following their own instinctive response to the need of other people, but it was Kitwood who gave us the narrative.[1]

Now – ten years later – the challenge is to achieve a critical mass of care staff so that isolated examples of good practice can become the mainstream. People have generally learned to 'talk the talk' – even the policy-makers (who generally trail far behind the practitioners). The *National*

Service Framework for Older People[2] has Standard Two devoted to person-centred care. The National Care Standards Commission is beginning to insist that care homes and home-care agencies deliver person-centred care.

But how do we make it happen? How do we learn to 'walk the walk' as well as 'talk the talk'? How do we help people who want to work with those with dementia to overcome the deep-seated resistance to engaging them at a truly personal level?

If we are going to stop people with dementia being treated as non-persons, we have to learn how to do this. 'A person becomes a person through other people.' Individual care workers in the field often realize that their innate commonsense approach is inadequate for dementia care. But this is all they have to bring to the job, in the absence of proper training. Families also hope for and expect to find more than physical care when they place their relatives in long-term care homes. Many search long and hard for homes that can provide more.

I am firmly on the side of those who believe that person-centred care can be achieved – even within the present budgetary constraints. To me, this is not just a practical but also a spiritual issue. Treating people as people rather than objects is a profoundly important spiritual task.

The study

1 Brief history of the project

The project was designed originally by Professor Tom Kitwood and started in January 1998. A team of three part-time researchers from Bradford Dementia Group started work – Errollyn Bruce, Claire Surr and myself. Kitwood had approached Methodist Homes for the Aged (as it was then known) and obtained funding from them to carry out a three-year longitudinal study in their homes. He did this because he viewed Methodist Homes as an organization which was committed to the idea of providing person-centred care.

Quality of life in institutions has been an enduring issue. Specific interest in the fate of older people in long-term care was kindled by Townsend's[3] groundbreaking study exposing the poor quality of life experienced by older people in care homes. This has remained a cause for concern, but it is only in the past ten years that people with dementia have been included in this agenda. Once deemed beyond well-being and quality of life, there is now good evidence that, like all of us, people with dementia need dignity, purpose and control.[4]

2 Aims of the project
- To look for evidence of well-being among the residents in the study.
- To identify factors associated with the maintenance of well-being; and risk factors for poor long-term outcomes.
- To contribute to our understanding of how the care environment affects well-being.

3 Participants
At the end of the preliminary work, we had a sample of 93 people living in ten different Methodist Homes, located in different parts of England and Wales. They were mostly very old. The average age was 84. The age range was 59 to 98, with relatively few residents under 80.

The dementia of the people ranged through mild and moderate to severe. The range of MMSE (Mini Mental State Examination) scores was from 0 to 20, with an average of nine. The test was used before the study started to select the subjects and at regular intervals thereafter. The Activities of Daily Living was variable – with an average of 31 on the Bristol ADL Scale (possible maximum on the scale is 55). The range was from 12 to 55.

4 Methods of study
Residents were divided into groups of five.

Staff in the selected homes were asked to complete a well-being profile and make brief notes about well-being for each person every month.

We (the research team) were in the homes for two days each visit, including an overnight stay.

At the end of each visit, field notes were typed up. Taped conversations with residents were transcribed and all the numerical data were entered into the computer for analysis.

Case reviews for each resident were carried out at the end of the 24 months of data collection. This entailed reading all the field notes and transcripts of interviews with residents and staff. We also looked at the scores and ratings for all the measures for each resident. We tried to work out which factors had been most influential on the person's well-being.

5 Well-being
A central concept in the study was that of well-being. This is regarded as an outcome of the delivery of person-centred care. When all the quantitative and qualitative data had been collected residents were allocated to one of three well-being groups – high, medium or low. Residents were assessed by care staff and researchers separately. We found a high degree of agreement – 83 per cent between the two sets of assessments. Graphs

were made of each person's well-being so that we could observe patterns over time. The majority of residents showed signs for well-being for 60 per cent or more of the time during the study period:

High	44.5 per cent
Medium	45.5 per cent
Low	10.0 per cent.
Two groups combined	90.0 per cent

This was a very small number of individuals.

Comparisons were made between the different groups on all the transcripts of interview which we looked at.

6 Mindsets

Field notes and conversation transcripts were coded for the mindsets which act as the underpinnings of well-being. (Mindsets were adapted from the 'Global States' developed by Kitwood and Bredin.) The mindsets are:

• Identity.
• Sense of control.
• Hope.
• Social confidence.

Where people had high well-being, it was much easier to spot evidence of the mindsets, and it was generally more difficult in those with low well-being.

For this paper I propose to concentrate only on identity and hope.

Findings of the study

Well-being and identity

People showed strong signs of identity by presenting themselves positively and being keen to talk about themselves. They made an impact on others by talking about past experiences. They were aware of their own place in the world. They expressed feelings about their relationships and social position, and opinions about beliefs and feelings. These showed that people were in touch with what they felt to be important, both good and bad. Expressing opinions shows an expectation that someone will take notice of what you say. Sharing your negative feelings suggests an assumption that your feelings will count. We did not assume that well-being had to be associated with people who are always happy and jolly. Nobody is happy all the time. It is more complex than that.

Well-being and hope

Hope was defined by Kitwood and Bredin as 'a confidence that some security will remain even when so many things are changing, both outside and within' and 'a sense that the future will, in some way, be good'. We kept to that broad definition.

Two areas of life seemed to be crucial in maintaining hope. These are finding comfort and security despite everything, and finding meaning in life and acceptance of death.

Hope clearly has a spiritual connotation, although most of the research team felt that it was important to separate this from religion.[5] For the factors which we found were associated with well-being and those which we found to be threats to well-being, see the Appendix.

The context of care

We identified three factors which helped to form the context within which care was provided.

1 A special atmosphere

This is very important, though elusive to define. We identified that it came from the Christian atmosphere. Several families who were not Christians had chosen Methodist Homes because of this. Relatives who had visited many homes looking for the right place often commented on the fact that there was something special about them. Some comments from relatives were:

- Love and care that goes far beyond legal requirements.
- What really matters is that it is loving (from the daughter of a resident who had been a lifelong communist).
- Outstanding kindness of the staff, their patience and affection.

2 A non-punishing place

All the homes – but particularly the specialist homes and those with specialist wings – created an undemanding environment. By this we meant one that relieves anxiety for people with dementia from many of the demands that are likely to cause anxiety or put them at risk. Many residents sense that things like organizing meals, paying bills, laundry, mail and gardening were being taken care of in the home. Apart from a few critical fellow residents, the people around were generally accepting of the typical disabilities of dementia. They did not expect clear speech, coherence, speed, agility and so on, and did not put people under pressure to meet normal standards. More importantly, they did not make people feel less fully human on account of their disabilities.

For many residents, the homes were much less punishing than the outside world, and this was significant in helping them to maintain a sense of being a competent, valuable member of a community with much to offer. Several families commented that their relatives had become less agitated and distressed since coming into care, something that the staff were aware of too.

3 A clear value system

It was interesting to note that the clear Christian value system was valued by most families, whether they came from the same tradition or not. The idea that right and wrong is important fitted with the outlook of the residents. Questions of meaning are of great interest to people reaching the end of life. They are definitely on the agenda of Methodist Homes.

There is a strong sense of community in the homes – which is probably characteristic of Methodism. Both residents and staff expect to join in activities if they are able. There was a clear sense, sometimes expressed in interviews, that one should make the effort to join in if others had made the effort to organize something. There is also a recognition that the group should try to accommodate the needs of individuals, as well as for individuals to fit in with the group.

These underpinnings seem to provide a good backdrop for work which helps people to hold on to the meanings which have been an anchor in their life, whatever they are. We found that, on the whole, the atmosphere in the homes was inclusive.

These three underpinnings are definitely supportive of person-centred care and likely to support well-being. The distinction between the spiritual and the religious was very important to those who designed the research. It was felt by Methodist Homes that they made a feature of good spiritual care – each home having its own dedicated chaplain, in-house services on Sundays, mid-week prayer and hymn-singing groups, as well as regular volunteers from the church.

The question was asked by the researchers whether religious care was actually being confused with spiritual care and whether some people could feel excluded by it. However, it seemed to me that while this was an issue for the research team, it was not really an issue for the people we were studying. In fact they would not have related to our attempts to separate the two. Most of the people in the study had spent their whole lives within a particular faith tradition – Christianity. The branch of it within which they lived was Methodism. It was part of the air they breathed and they would no more question its truths than they would doubt their own existence.

I came across a definition of spiritual well-being by Eileen Shamy which seemed to put into words what I want to say. The idea was also reflected back to me clearly in conversations with some of the residents in the study. In *More than Body, Brain and Breath* she said:

> Spiritual well-being is an affirmation of life in a relationship with God, self, community and the environment, that nurtures and celebrates wholeness. It is the strong sense that I am 'kept' and 'held' by Someone greater than myself who 'keeps' the whole of creation, giving it life and purpose. It is the certain knowledge that I am part of meaning and purpose.[6]

The role of faith

Finding meaning in life has long been identified as an important characteristic in survivors of extreme situations. There is no doubt that dementia may be classed as an extreme situation. Methodist Homes give a context of meaning which is familiar to many residents, and is particularly relevant to those for whom religious activities maintain continuity with their past religious involvement. Singing the old hymns, hearing familiar words, marking familiar landmarks throughout the Church's year, help many residents to feel they are in a good place, even if it is not home. Even for those who did not belong to this faith tradition, they were familiar to people of the oldest generation from their school days when everyone attended Christian school assemblies.

There was little doubt that the Christian environment encouraged reflectiveness, connectedness and meaning to life, attributes which are generally accepted as some of the secular or non-religious attributes of spirituality.

'A Special Kind of Care'

The final report of the research was published in November 2002. The title is intended to position the report clearly within the current political debate about the funding of long-term care. At present, far more people with dementia are being cared for in residential care homes than in nursing homes.

We wanted to give a clear message that, while people with dementia do not usually need nursing care, they definitely need more than mainstream residential care. They need staff who have received additional specialist training and a higher ratio of staff to residents than those without dementia.

The report can be downloaded from the MHA Care Group website at www.mha.org.uk.

What is implied by 'A Special Kind of Care'? The report emphasizes:

- an understanding of the particular disabilities and experiences of dementia;
- avoiding malignant social psychology;
- communication;
- interpretation;
- empowerment;
- help with grieving and emotional turmoil;
- making good use of life history;
- making use of external sources of support;
- spiritual care.

Some of the implications for practice arising from the study

- We need to provide people with dementia with opportunities for sustained conversation, where they can talk about themselves and their experiences.
- People with dementia need us to acknowledge and encourage their attempts to seek meaning as they try to make sense of their experiences. It is clear that they are making strenuous efforts to sustain their own well-being, and these need to be supported.
- Staff who are caring for people with low well-being, who seem to be overwhelmed by negative experiences, need a great deal of support.

Personal challenges

It seems to me that as a person of faith, nurtured in the Western Protestant tradition, there are certain questions which, working with dementia, I must face. The traditional teaching of the Church, from the early Christian fathers and St Thomas Aquinas onwards down the centuries, has been that 'God's grace is a gift which is only possible to a rational being'.

The Reformation theologians reframed these ideas, but still assumed that rationality must be present, when they said that 'the person must be aware of their sinfulness and need for Christ in order to enjoy a relationship of trust and obedience with Him'.[7] Even now we still 'find it difficult to move beyond the vocabulary of reason, for thinking, reading, reflecting and communicating – words and ideas – lie at the heart of so much Christian life'.[8] This has posed particular problems to those who minister to people with dementia whose ability to think, read, reflect and communicate becomes progressively impaired.

An alternative narrative came in the early years of the twentieth century from theologians Karl Barth and Martin Buber who developed theologies in which relationship rather than reason was understood as the cornerstone of being human. The 'I–Thou' relationship they called it, or – 'Umuntu ukumuntu ngybanye abantu' – 'a person becomes a person through other people'.

It is interesting that the idea of the 'I–Thou' relationship was a strong influence on Tom Kitwood's definition of the 'person-centred approach to dementia care'. It is still included in the course material for the BDG (Bradford Dementia Group) Certificate of Education in Dementia Studies.

This theology gives me an alternative to the statements which are so often made by family carers – 'The person I love died long ago'; 'All that is left of the person is an empty shell'; 'Dementia is the death which leaves the body behind' – in other words, 'the disaster view of dementia'.

I have to believe that there is purpose and meaning in life in order to go on. I'm with Anne Frank when she wrote in her diary, 'It is utterly impossible for me to build my life on a foundation of chaos, suffering and death'.[9]

The 'New Picture of Care' research provided me with clear evidence – in the form of transcripts of recorded conversations with people in the study and observations made about them by the staff – that their humanity is still intact. I have no doubt at all that I was engaging, sometimes at a deep level, as one human being with another human being. It made no difference that the other person had virtually no short-term memory and that their language skills were impaired. I know that we met – soul to soul.

Initially it was not easy to do this. We had concerns and questions about our own abilities. First, would the people be prepared to talk to us? Clearly they would not remember us, as we would only be visiting them at three-month intervals. So what cues could we give them to assist the process? What would we do if they had nothing at all to say to us? We learned how to do this – by trial and error – and I am so grateful that we did. Having these conversations is an experience for which I shall always be grateful.

To quote Eileen Shamy again, 'I know that one of the sweetest, most normalizing experiences any of us can have is that of sharing joy . . .

briefly we had entered each other's world, each with a crowd of associated memories'.[10]

To conclude, I should like to let a few of the people I talked to speak for themselves. Their names have been changed.

Miss Mills

I asked her (on my third visit), 'Miss Mills, do you pray?' 'Oh yes,' she said. 'Now that's something I couldn't do without. That is . . . that's always been part of my life. I had grandparents who were great . . . church members and I . . . they took me to church when I was small and I've always carried on. And that's been part of my life and that's that.' So I said, 'It's part of who you are, isn't it?', and she said, 'Really, yes. If people only realized that, it does become part of your own life . . . I was taken to school, to church, when I was much too young to understand, but I suppose we absorb it.'

Later, she said, 'It's good to have a laugh isn't it? . . . We live on laughter . . . when you think about it . . . we live a tremendous amount on laughter . . . there you are. We've got to live on something, so it might as well be laughter.' Later I asked her, 'So you have no worries about the future?' and she said, 'Oh no, no . . . I've been taken care of all this time and it will continue. It's nice to feel so safe.'

Miss Mills was 93. She also had very poor short-term memory but seemed to be happy doing very little. Her MMSE score was consistently 18. When I asked her if she looked back over her long life, she said, 'Yes, I suppose I . . . well it's . . . I mean I don't gloat over it, if you know what I mean but I . . . er . . . I do. If something reminds me of it, I either laugh or wonder what in the world was happening at that particular time . . . for that to happen.' I asked her, 'Are you still learning?' She said, 'I suppose so. If something happens I think . . . Ooh I don't think I've ever had that happen to me before. Which is learning.' 'And coming to live in a place like this?' 'I've never, ever experienced anything like it . . . but I'm very happy because you're learning something new.' Not a bad thing to feel when you're 93.

Jim Phillips

An excellent example of good spiritual and religious care was given by a man referred to as Jim Phillips in the report. Jim had a long career in the regular Army and retired with the rank of Major. He had also been a lifelong active member of the Church of Scotland and became a Sessions Clerk of the church on retirement. His cognitive impairment was too advanced for recorded conversation after the first visit when he told me that the home's dog was actually his dog and that he looked after him, remarking, 'Actually Paddy is a lot less trouble than anyone else as far as I can see because he keeps quiet. Fairly quiet . . . and he's a terribly nice dog.' (The fact that Paddy was actually a bitch with another name was never an issue for anyone, and Jim continued to think of her as his own.) He had brought up the children of two marriages; he was widowed twice, and obviously had a very strong need to look after and cherish the ladies – in the most gentlemanlike manner.

The chaplain of the specialist dementia home where he lived, who has made a particular study of ministry to people with dementia, realized that Jim had special needs. He was not accepting the dementia-adapted act of worship in the home and never joined in when it was held. The chaplain felt that Jim probably didn't even recognize that it was a religious service. So she arranged for a volunteer from the Methodist church in the local town to come every Sunday to collect Jim and take him to church.

I observed Jim at monthly intervals throughout the two years of the data collection, and he was always moving around the home, escorting someone or hovering, unable to concentrate on anything for more than a few minutes. He sat down only when he was really tired. According to the daily records at the home, it was regularly reported that he enjoyed the service and was always peaceful and calm afterwards.

Knowing, from observation, how hard it was for Jim to sit still for any length of time, I found this behaviour really difficult to explain. Therefore I asked the volunteer who took him to church about these visits. He assured me that Jim did sit through the service, which lasted well over an hour, including quite a long sermon. He joined in a lot of the hymns and prayers which he knew by heart and very much enjoyed the social time afterwards. I concluded that this weekly experience must be reinforcing his sense of connection with his Lord and his faith as well as with the wider community and gave him an extra sense of peace which enabled him to relax. It was definitely instrumental in maintaining his well-being.

Sister Janet

'I suppose I'm too old darling. I'm really getting very old now . . . and you can't stop it . . . you go on and on and there's nothing you can do to stop it' – Sister Janet and King Lear. She was 97 at the time, virtually blind and only able to walk with a frame guided by a care assistant. But she still wanted to be doing things for other people. 'I'm not used to this dull sort of existence,' she said. 'I'm bored. Yes. I've had a good life and I'm bored now . . . you've got to have some sort of . . . when I say job, I don't mean a paid job, you've got to have some purpose, something definite that you're doing . . . and you don't need money necessarily.' In fact, the reasons for her lack of activity were related to her physical disabilities rather than her dementia.

On another visit she was very fed up, but was able to describe her feelings about her mental state very accurately. 'I don't feel as though I'm me at all. I feel as though I'm some queer creature who's come to earth here, but who, I don't know. I don't know myself' (seventh visit). That seems to me to be a vivid description of the confusion caused by dementia . . . 'I hate this way of not knowing what to do next.'

On another occasion, when we were discussing what it was like living with other people all the time, she said, 'Living with other people doesn't make you feel less lonely, it makes you feel more lonely . . . if they're not people who belong to you.' Her moods changed of course, and on other occasions she was very protective of the home and told me how she felt loved and cared for by the staff.

On my second visit I asked her, 'Do you feel at peace and ready to depart?' and she said, 'I don't think about it. You just go on going on. At least that's what I do . . . why should I [speculate about the future]? I'm quite happy here and I'll be happy to go when the time comes.' When I said, 'You've always been a great believer, haven't you?' she said, 'Oh yes!! That's something different.'

She had virtually no short-term memory (her MMSE score was between 12 and 14). She would drink her favourite cup of black coffee, and almost as soon as it was finished would ask for another, saying she had not had a drink for ages. But she was still able to put into words the nuances of her feelings.

She was something of a hero in the Methodist church, having been one of the first deaconesses who went to work in the 'mission field' (the Caribbean). She was awarded the MBE for this work. By the time I met her she had absolutely no recollection or interest in that fact. Her chaplain said, 'She has worked extremely hard all her life. She is completely imbued with the Protestant work ethic and is bewildered to find herself in a situation where there is nothing she can do.' Her key worker – a young man of African descent – told me, 'She is a most special person to me and I love her.'

I think that says it all. It answers the question of King Lear with which we began. 'Who is it that can tell me who I am?' It is people like him who can say, 'She is a most special person . . . and I love her.'

Notes

1 Kitwood, T., 'The Dialectics of Dementia: With Particular Reference to Alzheimer's Disease', *Ageing and Society,* 10, 1990, pp. 177–96.
2 Department of Health, *National Service Framework for Older People,* 2001.
3 Townsend, P., *The Last Refuge: A Survey of Residential Institutions and Homes for the Aged in England and Wales,* Routledge and Kegan Paul, 1962.
4 Bruce, E., Surr, C. and Tibbs, M. A., *A Special Kind of Care,* MHA Care Group, 2002.
5 Ibid.
6 Shamy, E., *More than Body, Brain and Breath,* ColCom Press, 1997.
7 Saunders, J., *Dementia: Pastoral Theology and Pastoral Care,* Grove Books, 2002.
8 Ibid.
9 Anne Frank, cited by Shamy, 1997.
10 Ibid.

References

Kitwood, T. and Bredin, K., 'Towards a Theory of Dementia Care: Personhood and Well-being' in *Ageing and Society,* 12, 1992, pp. 269-87.
Packer, T., 'Does Person-centred Care Exist?' *Journal of Dementia Care,* May/June, 2000, pp. 19–21.
Shakespeare, William, *Arden Shakespeare: King Lear,* third series, Foakes, R. A. (ed.), Thomson Learning, 2001.
Shenk, D., *The Forgetting: Understanding Alzheimer's: A Biography of a Disease,* HarperCollins, 2001.

Appendix

The following factors were identified in *A Special Kind of Care.*

1 Factors associated with high well-being

As a group, compared to those with moderate or low well-being, they:

- were less disabled;
- had lower levels of cognitive impairment;
- were more independent in activities of daily living;
- had better language and better communication skills (we made a clear distinction between the two);
- were healthier than others;
- showed fewer signs of depression;
- had fewer problems with bowels or skin;
- had fewer problems with incontinence or mobility;
- were more active physically and socially.

All these factors are obviously associated with better physical health and less advanced cognitive impairment and might easily be predicted.

However, there were other factors which were more surprising. The group who showed high well-being also:

- had better relationships with their families;
- had more supporters who were making strenuous efforts to meet their needs;
- seemed to cope better when faced with cognitive decline and/or a change in their abilities;
- participated in a greater range of activities on a regular basis;
- were more sociable and had more friendships with specific people;
- spent a lot of time moving about the home;
- had more favourable relationships;
- were getting more than average amounts of time from the staff;
- were more likely to be seen as popular or seen as characters;
- were less likely to have their emotional needs overlooked by the staff;
- were less likely to have no visitors at all;
- were less likely to have inappropriate support from people unable to understand their dementia.

2 Factors associated with threats to well-being
- Accumulated losses and emotional turmoil.
- The experience of dementia and the disabilities it brings.
- Changed relationships.
- Living in community in long-term care.
- Having to accept help with personal care.
- Ill-health and physical decline.
- Depression.
- Sedative medication.
- Negative life events.

Chapter 5

Learning Love from People with Dementia

JOHN KILLICK

John Killick was formerly writer-in-residence for Westminster Health Care. In this chapter he shows us how much we have to learn from listening to the wisdom of the vulnerable. He shows us how it is possible to establish and maintain meaningful relationships with people living with dementia. His work holds together the head and the heart and he demonstrates the power and possibility of poetry as a way of accessing our spiritual world. He illustrates this with moving poems from people whom he has interviewed.

Not much more than a decade ago, the whole future for people with dementia looked bleak indeed. The medical model held sway, and since doctors and scientists didn't know what caused the condition, how to predict who might get it and who might not, and there was no cure in sight, they threw up their hands intellectually and looked the other way. Here is a typical definition:

> As a result of a degenerative process in the brain, nerve cells become gradually incapable of communicating with one another. The disintegration of the brain tissue leads to a breaking of the communication lines which anchor a person in his own time and environment. His mind goes adrift. Communication with other people and even his own body becomes disturbed. There is total dislocation. The patient slowly but inevitably regresses to the functional level of an ailing, helpless newborn baby.[1]

Some threw up their hands emotionally too:

> There is this grotesque thing in the corner . . . an uncollected corpse that the undertaker cruelly forgot to take away.[2]

Unfortunately the perpetrator of that second quote also happened to be President of the Alzheimer's Disease Society at the time!

Then along came Tom Kitwood of Bradford University to turn the whole scene on its head. He proposed to replace the old formula:

Person with DEMENTIA

by:

PERSON with dementia

This changes the perspective dramatically. Instead of looking at the disease as dominating the person, we see the person first and the condition second, as one would with cancer or tuberculosis. The problem with dementia, of course, and the reason why that had not been proposed before, is that it attacks cognitive capacity, as many other diseases do not, and therefore was thought to impair the very sense of self by which we distinguish and value the human. Many family carers still speak of their loved one as having 'gone away', but this may be a misperception caused by the communication difficulties which are a common characteristic of the condition. Similarly the 'challenging behaviours' which many people with dementia are supposed to exhibit may be the natural consequence of the misunderstanding and resulting mistreatment of the person by those around them. This is the psychosocial model of dementia which Kitwood expounded, and it led to the concept of 'person-centred care', where everyone is to be treated as an individual despite the severity of the symptoms exhibited.

This is, of course, a counsel of perfection, and Kitwood acknowledged that it posed an uncommon challenge for those called upon to face it:

As we discover the person who has dementia we also discover something of ourselves. For what we ultimately have to offer is not technical expertise but ordinary faculties raised to a higher level: our power to feel, to give, to stand in the shoes (or sit in the chair) of another.[3]

The crucial phrase here is 'ordinary faculties raised to a higher level'. Therein lies the problem: how many people can achieve that degree of empathy, and how do you learn to exercise it? Faith Gibson in an important article raises the same dilemma, but answers it in a way which makes plain that once one realizes that communication is possible, there is really no alternative but to engage with it:

We must employ whatever power we have in the world of dementia care for this purpose (risking person-centred communication). We must use our present knowledge, our skills and feelings, to communicate. We are morally obliged to continue working in extending our limited understanding, developing our embryonic skills, and taming our deep anxieties.[4]

One of the barriers to empowering persons with dementia is the value our society places on intellectual capacity. Most of our institutions (notably our education system) enshrine reason as the moving force of society, and financial rewards come to those who can harness it to provide for people's needs in the most efficient manner. Stephen Post, an American ethicist, has coined the term 'hypercognitive culture' for the shrine at which we worship:

> We live in a culture that is the child of rationalism and capitalism, so clarity of mind and economic productivity determine the value of a human life . . . Rather than allowing declining mental capacities to divide humanity into those who are worthy or unworthy of full moral attention, it is better to develop an ethics based on the essential unity of human beings and on an assertion of equality despite unlikeness of mind.[5]

Children and older people miss out on this scale of values, but we are prepared to put faith and resources in the way of the former because of what they may become. The latter have outlived their usefulness, and people with dementia are at the bottom of the pile because they are potentially a drain upon the national budget, and time and money spent on them are not going to be recouped in any way.

Into this negative scenario I want to introduce some tentative suggestions of what people with dementia may have to offer us which may have been overlooked. First of all there is emotional honesty. Although it is undoubtedly true that many of those with the condition are caught out and left floundering by our emphasis on cause and effect and our insistence on the importance of maintaining the chain of memory, their ability to live intensely in the present seems to be something special from which we could learn. This gives a particular resonance to new relationships, but it also means that our motives are quite keenly put on trial. Quite often in communicating with individuals I have felt that I am being observed, tested and somehow found wanting. It is uncomfortable to be put in this position but also productively challenging. In a remarkable paragraph, Debbie Everett, a hospital chaplain in Canada, has identified this aspect of communication as follows:

People with dementia are magic mirrors where I have seen my human condition, and have repudiated the commonly held societal values of power and prestige that are unreal and shallow. Because people with dementia have their egos stripped from them, their unconscious comes very close to the surface. They in turn show us the masks behind which we hide our authentic personhood from the world.[6]

Another aspect closely allied to integrity which I can identify is that of spiritual awareness. In some, this can seem a striving for grace; in others, it is as if this quality has been vouchsafed to them almost because of a lack of effort, as a kind of gift for humility. An example of the former would be the following poem dictated to me by a man who always conveyed the impression of being very much concerned about such matters:

> to see what is beautiful
> to hear what is beautiful
> they don't know what is beautiful –
> all these young people
> good men, nice boys, fine chaps –
> they are too busy to see
> it'll be a good bit longer
> before *you* see
> what you want to see
> but they don't want to see
> what in some queer way
> they are anxious to see
> we see it very rarely
> but the difference is
> *we are trying to see!*[7]

When I asked for a title for the piece, he suggested 'Glimpses'. The next poem was dictated by a man who had never previously revealed to me feelings of this nature, though he did have moments of quiet reflection, usually quickly superseded by episodes of boisterous humour. On this occasion he had appeared asleep, when he suddenly opened his eyes, asked me if I had my notebook with me, and unhesitatingly spoke the following words:

> In the skies up high
> with the clouds below you –
> that's where I'd like to be.
> With the birds,

the little sparrows,
but I'll remain a man.
It's an attraction,
it's the spaces
that we can't reach.
I was up there one day
and got the sensation
I didn't want to come down.
I'd rather be
a creature of the air
than of the earth.[8]

When I asked this man for a title, he replied scornfully, "The Blue Far Yonder" of course', as if no other would do. The first poem is more mysterious, the second simpler, at least on the surface. What they both have in common is a sense of reaching out, a visionary quality, which I find distinctive and moving.

One day I was in a nursing-home lounge and noticed a lady in the corner of the room who was quietly singing to herself. It was a low, sweet sound. I asked the staff if this was unusual. 'No, she does it all the time. She's the happiest soul on the Unit', one of them said, and the others concurred. When I had made contact with the lady, and gained her permission to listen closely to her words, this was what I wrote down:

I don't know what to do – I want to go home – I can sit here but – I don't seem happy any more – I don't know what to do – I want to but – I can't any more – I want to lay – I don't know when it will be – I want so let me have it – Don't make it so hard for me – O world, I don't know what to do – I want to see my sunset good – I want it as it was promised – I'm waiting for the hour – I want to see my sunset good.[9]

There are two striking aspects of this text. First, the complete mismatch between the impression of the lady's singing and the message contained in the words. This 'happiest soul on the Unit' was in fact longing for death, and the message this conveys to care staff could not be starker: unless they pay attention to the minutiae of communication, they are never going to come close to understanding the states of mind of those they are looking after. Second, though the feelings expressed are largely negative, the lady does have expectations that death, when it comes, will bring her spiritual release: 'I want to see my sunset good' shows faith in an ultimately positive resolution of life's journey.

I return to the largest of all the big issues posed by dementia: what the condition does to the person. Here are two answers, both given by individuals with Alzheimer's disease. In her book, *Who Will I Be When I Die?*, the Australian Christine Boden writes:

> The unique essence of 'me' is at my core, and this is what will remain with me at the end. I will be perhaps more truly 'me' than I have ever been.[10]

And the American Barb Noon says this in her poem 'Burning Bright':

> Sometimes I picture myself like a candle.
> I used to be a candle about eight feet tall – burning bright. Now, every day I lose a little bit of me.
> Someday the candle will be very small. But the flame will be just as bright.[11]

At Stirling University we have produced books, packs and videos to encourage the use of the arts with people with dementia. There is a video titled *Responding to Music*, and in one of the interactions the man with dementia says to the musician: 'You have touched the strings at the very centre of my heart'.[12] I truly believe that people with dementia have the capacity to do that for us if we can only stifle our anxieties, lose some of our self-consciousness, and let love accomplish its amazing transformations.

Notes

1 Souren, L. and Franssen, E., *Broken Connections: Alzheimer's Disease*, Swets and Zeitlinger, 1994, p. 14.

2 Miller, J., 'Goodbye to All This', *Independent on Sunday*, 15 April 1990.

3 Kitwood, T., 'Discover the Person, Not the Disease', *Journal of Dementia Care*, 1 (6), 1993, pp. 16–17.

4 Gibson, F., 'Unmasking Dementia', *Community Care Supplement*, 29 October/ 3 November 1999, p. 24.

5 Post, S., *The Moral Challenge of Alzheimer's*, Johns Hopkins University Press, 1994.

6 Everett, D., *Forget Me Not: The Spiritual Care of People with Alzheimer's Disease*, Inkwell Press, 1996, p. 167.

7 Killick, J. and Cordonnier, C., *Openings: Dementia Poems and Photographs*, Hawker Publications, 2001.

8 Ibid.

9 Benson, S. and Killick, J., *Creativity in Dementia Care Calendar 2003*, Hawker Publications, 2002.

10   Boden, C., *Who Will I Be When I Die?*, HarperCollins, 1997, pp. 49–50.
11   Noon, B., in S. Benson and J. Killick, *Creativity in Dementia Care Calendar 2004*, Hawker Publications, 2003.
12   Mullan, M. and Killick, J., *Responding to Music*, Dementia Services Development Centre, University of Stirling, 2001.

Chapter 6

Rediscovering the Person through Shared Memories

GAYNOR HAMMOND

Gaynor Hammond is a member of the Christian Council on Ageing Dementia Group and a trained nurse who has been project worker for the Faith in Elderly People, Leeds Dementia Project, since 1998. Her particular interests are the spiritual needs of people with dementia, reminiscence and the Memory Box.

Many people have found reminiscence a very useful tool for helping to open up those windows of recognition with people whose memories have been lost. I was on my way to do some reminiscence work with one of my local day centres. I had plenty of time to spare and decided to call at the hairdresser's for a trim. When I arrived, he asked me if I would like a colour – it wouldn't take long and he was anxious that his trainee, who had been learning to colour hair, got some experience. I was in a charitable mood that day so I agreed. I am a natural blond but need a little help these days to keep it that way, so what could go wrong? He then asked me if I would give her free rein in choice of colour, assuring me that she had a good eye for this and he wanted to encourage her. This girl was seventeen! Warning bells started to ring, but again I was assured that, if I didn't like it, it would wash out. I relaxed and let her loose. The result was Belisha-beacon yellow. I couldn't believe what I had let her do, and I was now due to go to the day centre so had no time to do anything about it. My only consolation was that I was working with people with dementia, so they probably wouldn't notice!

I walked into the room. People had begun to arrive and were sitting in a semi-circle staring vacantly into space. Some were confused and disorientated by the journey from home.

I began to converse with them, helping them through reality orientation to connect with where they were. 'Hello,' I said breezily, 'welcome to the day centre. It's Wednesday morning. My name is Gaynor and I am here to do some memory work with you. We are going to . . .' A voice from the corner brought me up sharply. 'My hair used to be that colour.' Oh no, my hair! 'You'll never believe what I did', and I began to relate the whole story of letting a seventeen-year-old loose on my hair, ending with the words, 'I must have been mad!' How insensitive can you get. I had just said I must have been mad to a group of people with dementia. With my head in my hands I was mentally writing out my resignation. I was clearly unfit for this job.

As I looked up, everyone was laughing and one by one they started to relate their own hair disaster stories and we spent the next hour laughing till we ached. No one walking into that room would have suspected that anyone there was suffering from dementia. That became our reminiscence session for the day. And if you are really serious about this work, then I recommend that you go straight to the hairdresser's and ask for Belisha-beacon yellow!

What I want to describe to you is the Memory Box. There is a wonderful book[1] about a little boy called Wilfrid Gordon McDonald Partridge and his search for the meaning of 'memory'. In his search he asks five of his friends, who are all much older than him, to explain the word 'memory'. These are the answers they gave:

Something warm.
Something from long ago.
Something that makes you cry.
Something that makes you laugh.
Something as precious as gold.

One question, five answers and, yes, memory is all of those things. If only there was a way of wrapping up all those precious, sad, funny, warm and golden moments and putting them in a box to keep for ever, to unpack and relive once again, whenever we wanted – now that would be a gift worth having.

Studies have shown that the attitude of carers towards a person can be radically altered by some knowledge of the person's life history. The experience of Age Exchange and writers on reminiscence, notably Faith Gibson, confirm this view.

So if general reminiscence is so valuable, how much more would personal reminiscence be? That is why we at Faith in Elderly People, Leeds looked at the idea of capturing people's personal reminiscences through creating a personal Memory Box.

Everything we have done in life – the places we have lived and the people we have encountered – have had some effect or influence on us and helped to make us the people we are. As we go through life we build up a personal history with a mixture of joys and pleasures. This Memory Box would contain a collection of personal mementoes to use as memory cues to open up those 'windows of recognition' and therefore help the person to retain their identity.

The best way I can explain the Memory Box is to show you mine.

Here is a stone and a seashell collected from Blackpool beach. I was born and brought up in Blackpool, so it is a very special place to me. I have photographs of me in Blackpool, me on a donkey, me swimming in the sea. Perhaps I had luminous hair then – Sellafield nuclear power station being just round the corner!

Though photos are good and need to be included, the shell and pebble are tactile, tangible reminders of glorious days spent on the beach. Whenever I show this to older people, particularly those with dementia, it is amazing how many lift the shell up to their ear, to listen to the sea!

My working days were spent as a nurse. Here I have my frill cap, belt and badges. The uniform was very important to me, as it was to all of us. We were very proud of it, and the nurses of that era rebelled when we had to trade it in for something more practical. I can remember clearly the day the hospital where I was working closed down and I had to move to one of the large NHS hospitals. They gave me a pair of pyjamas to wear. It was awful and, even worse, when I arrived on the ward almost all the nurses had piercing everywhere! Would I have to do that to fit in? I think it was then that I decided my nursing days were over.

But uniform is very important. A practice nurse goes to visit an elderly couple to make sure they are managing all right. The husband cares for his wife with dementia. She is what is often termed 'pleasantly confused', which in effect means she sits there most of the day and does nothing and she causes no trouble. Except when the practice nurse visits. Then she comes alive. The uniform of navy-blue dress and belt with buckle and badges sparks memories of when she was a nurse, and once more she is back in her role. The husband is sent off to make tea. It has to be brought in on a tray with cups and saucers. 'Sister' is invited to sit down, and tales of patients and work are told for the next half-hour. Such is the power of memory triggers.

I have a baby-gro in my box; this was worn by my eldest son who is now 26. He is not happy that I have kept it, so I dare not tell him of all the booties, matinee coats and other garments that I have kept. But this baby-gro is symbolic of all the children who have enriched my life.

Hobbies are important. In my box I have a paint palette, brush and two small paintings. I love water-colour painting. Hopefully, if you have to look after me, you will just need to produce paper and paints and you can keep me quiet and out of trouble for hours.

In her book,[2] Eileen Shamy spoke about her mother who had dementia. Her mother loved to crochet, and even in the late stages of dementia she would spend many fulfilling hours employed in this hobby. That is, until the day she lost her crochet hook. It had only fallen under her chair and she had a spare in her bedside table, but the nurses were always too busy to look and eventually it got forgotten. When her daughter Eileen went to visit, she was distraught to find that her mother had been robbed of the skill which had given her so much pleasure. All for the few minutes it would have taken to find her hook!

I keep a lipstick in my box. This is because make-up is important to me. It is a part of my routine. I get up, take a shower, get dressed then put on my make-up. The lipstick is there to remind anyone who might be looking after me that I don't want to appear in public without my make-up!

We have a wonderful psychiatrist who is very sensitive to people's needs and always looks at their spiritual needs and person-centred care before prescribing pills. One day she was sent for by a nursing home and asked to prescribe some sedative for a resident who was presenting challenging behaviour. In other words, she wouldn't go down to breakfast and was thumping any nurse who tried to make her. When the doctor arrived, she immediately noticed that the lady, who was usually heavily made up, had no make-up on, so she asked why. She was told that the lady's daughter took it all away because she was looking like a clown! The doctor prescribed more make-up and a nurse was sent to the chemist to replenish her stock. Once made up, the lady went down to breakfast with no trouble, happy because that spiritual need had been recognized.

I have many other things in my box, but finally I will show you my Bible. I am a Christian, and for me my faith infiltrates every part of my life. So Bible reading, prayer and fellowship of other Christians are important to me. I was working in a nursing home, and one of the residents had been a Methodist local preacher. He now had dementia, and one of the ways the disease affected him was that he shouted and swore a lot – much to the dismay of his family and care workers. But instead of affirming him, the fact that he had been a lay preacher was used against him. He was asked on a regular basis, 'Is this how ministers carry on?' One morning I offered to get him up. When I approached him, I introduced myself, told him it was morning and suggested that he might like to get up. He told me to go away – or words to that effect! I ignored this but said to him, 'I hear you were a lay preacher, I am a Christian too, shall we start the day with prayer?' He said, 'I'd like that.' A sentence without swearing! So I took his prayer book out of his drawer and read one of the Psalms. He recited it with me, not needing to look at the prayer book for he knew the words. He had probably started his day with prayer and Bible reading for years, so this was ministering to his spirituality, and it was a precious moment for us both as we worshipped together. I then got him out of bed and washed and dressed him without the usual struggle but in a peaceful state of mind and spirit.

I spoke to the nurses later and suggested that they read a Psalm from the Bible with him before they started to get him up. One said it would take too long – even though it took two of them much longer to get him up than it had taken one of me. Another said she didn't believe the Bible. I did point out to her that I had seen her reading a tabloid newspaper to a resident, and she couldn't surely believe in that – but it didn't stop her doing it!

I hope that describing my Memory Box has encouraged you to engage with people through reminiscence and to help them develop their own Memory Box as a means of maintaining their own identity.

Notes

1   Fox, M., *Wilfrid Gordon McDonald Partridge*, Picture Puffin, 1987.
2   Shamy, E., *A Guide to the Spiritual Dimension of Care for People with Alzheimer's Disease and Related Dementia: More than Body, Brain and Breath*, Jessica Kingsley, 2003.

Chapter 7

Connecting with the Whole Person through Activities

SALLY KNOCKER

Sally Knocker uses her professional expertise as a freelance dementia special-
ist trainer and writer to remind us of the importance of purposeful activity
for all older people. The needs of people with dementia are considerably
transformed, she suggests, through time, attention, human contact, conversa-
tion and a friendly smile. I have learnt from many organizations of the way
Sally has lifted the ambitions of care through enabling them to think differ-
ently about what purposeful and meaningful activity means. In particular,
in this chapter she looks at the work of Tom Kitwood in this area and
concludes that this should be an important ministry for churches.

This chapter is written with me wearing two 'hats'. The first is as project
manager for 'Growing with Age', a NAPA (National Association for
Providers of Activities for Older People) project which is exploring the
extent to which residents in care homes and sheltered housing can be
more closely integrated with the life of the wider community, which of
course includes the church community. The other 'hat' I wear is as a
specialist in the area of dementia care over the last twelve years and with
a particular passion for promoting activities.

The focus of this chapter is to explore a little what we think people
with dementia might need and to touch on what members of faith communities might offer individuals as part of a wider definition of pastoral
care.

Some time ago I saw in the *Guardian* a 'Clare in the community'
cartoon by Harry Venning. It shows Clare visiting an old lady sitting in
her chair in a residential home. 'Crikey, Nan!' she says. 'Look at the time!
Sorry I've gone on, but it's been such a long time since my last visit, and I
had so much to tell you!' 'Don't you dare apologise!' says the old lady. 'I

get so few visitors here in the Home that I love to hear about you, that lovely boyfriend Brian, little Megan, naughty Ross the dog and all those clients that keep you so busy. But I agree, it has been a long time since your last visit . . . because I'm not your Nan. She's in the room next door.'

This cartoon makes a very significant point to me about what people living in care homes badly need. Most residents are not asking for lots of different group activities like quizzes, games or arts and crafts. Very few of us choose to spend large amounts of our time in large groupings in fact. Most of us live in couples or small families or alone. It is therefore not very surprising that what most older people long for is more *one-to-one time* and companionship. Time, attention, human contact, conversation, a friendly smile – these are the most important gifts we can offer people who feel isolated and possibly cut off from the home and community to which they belonged before they came to live in a care home. To me, this is an even more important ministry than churches offering opportunities for services for worship and Communion to people in care homes.

I turn now more specifically to what people with dementia might need from those who support them. Two short anecdotes of people with dementia with whom I have worked help illustrate the kinds of things that liven up people's lives, depending on their personality, background and interests.

The first point to make is that what people with dementia often need is much the same as what all of us need from life.

Normal everyday experiences

We can take many of these things for granted, but getting milk out of the fridge for a cup of tea, travelling in a car or a bus, watching children playing, experiencing the changes in weather, or enjoying the spring blossom and hearing the birds sing, can all enrich our lives and can some-times be sadly lacking for people living in institutional settings.

Variety in the day and not feeling bored

We all know that sitting for a whole day, at a series of seminars for example, looking in the same direction and passively listening to speakers, is not the most comfortable thing to do, and it is difficult to keep your concentration and interest. The old saying 'Variety is the spice of life' is particularly true for older people with dementia whose days will be much improved by not just sitting, but moving around, watching and doing different things, enjoying a range of things with which to engage.

To feel loved and needed

This is such a simple but important thing, and yet for many older people whose families are perhaps not so close at hand and who are no longer working, it is hard to feel that you still have a role which is valued in the world. Helping people to continue to feel needed can be done in such simple ways. I recently took a range of wedding hats and outfits into a care home and spent a very enjoyable half-hour consulting a small group of residents about which they felt suited me best for a wedding I was going to attend! I got some very forthright comments, and some interesting discussions about fashion and social etiquette at weddings ensued. But the most significant aspect of this activity was possibly that I was giving a message to those involved that I still respected their opinion; they *mattered to me* and I wanted to hear what *they had to say*.

Conversation and company

This is one of the most precious activities of all, and one where the churches surely have a precious resource in terms of the members of the congregation who can offer this friendship and fellowship.

Treats and fun to spice up life

All too often in care homes, all the fun is concentrated at Christmas time when everyone is inundated (and probably fairly exhausted) with festivities, good food, jolly music and so on. Why not bring aspects of these things more into everyday life – a chocolate or a nice drink or the fun of singing can make any day feel special!

When looking at the whole area of activities, I think it is also helpful to consider what people's deeper psychological needs might be and how engaging with activities can help us connect with the whole person. 'Doing' to many people is synonymous with being alive, making something happen and leaving their mark on the world. However, what does meeting a 'person's psychological needs' really mean? What actually are these needs?

The psychologist Tom Kitwood has described a cluster of needs, which overlap, coming together in the central need for love. The fulfilment of one of these needs will, to some extent, involve the fulfilment of the others as they are closely interrelated.

We will look at each of these psychological needs in turn, with a particular emphasis on how they might relate to a person engaged in an activity.

The need for comfort

The word 'comfort' carries meanings of tenderness, closeness and the soothing of pain or sorrow. To provide comfort to another person is to provide a kind of warmth and strength, which might support them at a time of need. In a very real sense a person who has dementia is likely to be experiencing loss and change and to be in need of these qualities.

There are many activities which might bring comfort to a person, particularly those which involve contact with others, for example receiving a hug from a child, holding someone's hand or possibly stroking a dog. Soaking in a warm bubble-bath or having a gentle hand-massage may also be comforting for some. Others might derive comfort from participation in a religious ritual or looking at the photograph of a loved one.

The need for attachment

In the field of child psychology there is a considerable body of theory which considers the importance of specific bonds of attachment for a young baby or child, given the vulnerability and uncertainty which is implicit in growing up and discovering the world. In a different but comparable way, a person with dementia might also be experiencing considerable uncertainty and new 'strange' situations, and so the need for the sense of safety and security that attachment can bring can be very heightened.

The attachments which people with dementia develop might not always be with particular people. It is quite common for a person's attachment needs to be expressed in terms of a quite intense preoccupation with a particular item like a handbag or keys or a piece of clothing. It might be very important, for example, for a woman to be able to sort through her handbag as a regular activity to reinforce a sense of security and control over her life, and for that handbag to never be far out of sight.

The need for identity

All of us will have different ways of describing our identity. For some people we may well define ourselves first in relation to our roles with others, for example 'I am a mother', or 'I am a wife'. Others may place greater emphasis on their race, nationality, religion or sexuality: 'I am Christian', 'I am Nigerian', 'I am gay'. For others, their sense of identity is strongly linked to the job that they do: 'I'm a builder', 'I'm a lawyer' – or the interests that they have: 'I love art', 'I enjoy walking'. To know who one is as a unique individual gives a sense of continuity with our past; and a 'story' or picture to present to others about what it is that matters to us can mean much.

It becomes especially important to respect a person's identity in the face of cognitive impairment. It is vital that we know enough about a person's life history to help hold their sense of identity if and when an individual's memory is failing. This is why things like developing a Memory Box as Gaynor has vividly described (in Chapter 6) or life history books or photo albums are so important.

The need for inclusion

Human beings are traditionally social animals who tend to live and work more in group situations or communities rather than operate in isolation. People with dementia continue to have this need to 'belong' in a group, yet can often find themselves feeling isolated even in a crowd. It is this need which is the central focus of the 'Growing with Age' project which seeks to include residents in homes within the wider community. Churches too can do a great deal to ensure a philosophy of inclusion in the way they welcome and support people with dementia, not just on Sundays, but in other aspects of the church community.

The need for occupation

This psychological need is the one that relates most obviously to involvement in activity. To be occupied means to be involved in the process of life in a way that is personally significant and which draws on a person's abilities and powers. A person might be occupied in the company of others, or in solitude, in obvious action, in reflection or in relaxation. What is important is that in whatever it is they are involved, they feel some sense of engagement and satisfaction rather than boredom or apathy.

Many of the ways in which people are most commonly occupied in daily life become less accessible to older people in care settings, for example tidying up your house, going out to a shop, or choosing to put your feet up and read a newspaper. Sometimes a person with dementia will seek out ways of being occupied by walking about a great deal or picking objects up or playing continuously with an item of clothing.

The skill of a care worker is to know when this kind of activity is an expression of boredom or frustration or when a person seems happily absorbed in the occupation. If the person does seem positively occupied, it is most important that a person is not disrupted or that the behaviour is not falsely labelled as either problematic or without meaning.

It might be argued that all these psychological needs relate to and connect with an individual's spiritual well-being. The definition of 'spiritual well-being' used by many practioners as 'moments of awe and wonder', 'experiences of life which transport one beyond the mundane' and 'relationships with others that give meaning and purpose in life' offer us an invitation to find simple activities which bring people these possibilities.

I can think of a number of examples of where these 'moments', 'experiences' and 'relationships' have been discovered: an afternoon spent 'wedding watching' sitting on a bench near a church on a sunny Saturday afternoon, enjoying the colours, laughter and sense of occasion of an event which reminded onlookers of their own special day. Another memory I have is of spending over half an hour with an older woman saying the Rosary while she was sitting on the loo. (I'm sure God didn't mind, as it provided her with some comfort!) Another memory is of reading aloud from a crossword puzzle book at the bedside of a man with dementia who had hardly spoken for months. When I said, 'Bird of prey – five letters', a clear voice emerged from the frail figure with the closed eyes in bed, 'Eagle!' Let us never make assumptions about what people with dementia can and cannot do. By giving the gift of time and helping people to feel occupied, included, respected and loved, the Church has a very special ministry to offer those who have dementia.

I would like to end with the vision of the 'Growing with Age' project and invite you to help contribute to making this vision a reality in future:

Imagine a world where the local residential home or sheltered housing scheme was the hub of community activity in an area, with doors open to a wealth of interesting experiences inside and outside the home – a place that people enjoy visiting rather than dread that they might end up there.

Note

Parts of this paper have been drawn from previous publications by Sally Knocker: *The Alzheimer's Society Book of Activities*, The Alzheimer's Society, 2002 and an article for *Signpost* 8 (3), February 2004, pp. 6–8.

Worshipping with People with Dementia

Chapter 8

Worshipping with Those with Dementia

PATRICIA HIGGINS and RICHARD ALLEN

In this chapter the authors prove that we need more practitioners to write about their experience. The reader is carefully guided through the principles to be followed when planning a service of worship, looking at practical considerations to be taken into account. A short section also considers the application of this philosophy to other faiths.

It used to be the case that one could walk into any Christian church or chapel and hazard a realistic guess at its denomination merely by observing the shape and style of the worship. This is probably no longer the case. The twentieth-century liturgical movement has brought about many changes. Not the least of these is a conscious integration of the ministry of pastoral care with one of the principles of the movement – that the activity of worship is 'the work of the people' and not something mysterious that is the exclusive tenure of the clergy.

From the Christian perspective, within any care setting, pastoral, spiritual and religious care come together when individuals meet to express their faith in formal or informal ways. This may take the form of impromptu prayer, a blessing, an anointing or a formal act of worship. Sensitive and effective pastoral ministry can only play its vital part at this juncture if the nature of the encounter is both appropriate to the needs of the individuals (which may in practice be very diverse) and facilitates an encounter with the realm of the 'Other'.

One of the advantages that a chaplain has over a parish visitor (in each case the lay or ordained status is immaterial) lies in the regular contact that he or she has with those to whom he or she is ministering. The more regular the contact, the greater the understanding of the pastoral, spiritual and religious needs is likely to be. However, one of the pits into which a chaplain can subconsciously fall is to assume that he or she can assess an individual's needs without first getting to know the setting or even meeting the individual concerned. The people who know the patients or clients most intimately will be those who care for them – family, friends, nurses, carers. So in the preparation of any programme of spiritual and religious care, the starting point for 'the work of the people' lies with this group.

In the case of the Candlelight Group, such collaboration was a natural adjunct to the nature of the regular pastoral work at the day hospital. At the outset of the project, identifying the needs of the group, defining the objectives of the project and establishing a means of measuring its effectiveness were identified as essential principles. The subsequent conversations between the chaplain and the nursing team leader, prior to designing the act of worship, for the most part avoided false starts and the necessity for major changes or revisions in the liturgy over the 4½ years that the Group has run.

Identifying the needs of the group

The onset and development of dementia brings with it changes in circumstances that move those who are affected from lives of normal social contact and relationship into ones where verbal communication becomes increasingly difficult. Responses to everyday situations can appear illogical, and the social pressure to withdraw, to save the embarrassment of oneself and others, is often too strong to resist. Increasing isolation is thus almost inevitable, accompanied by emotions of frustration, bewilderment and anger, implicitly seeking answers to questions such as, 'Why is this happening to me?' and 'Where is this leading?' One of the challenges presented to carers by such circumstances is to locate the thread that starts with the provision of pastoral care, moves into areas of spiritual care where such existential questions can begin to be addressed, and ultimately finds religious expression in the ritual activity that can shape some answers.

It has long been recognized that day centres and day hospitals, as well as the recreational and therapeutic activities in residential facilities, help to keep at bay the tendency towards isolation. But, by their very definition, group encounters only enable limited participation from each member. While recognizing the time constraints, there is no substitute for individual conversation, a time when love can be given and received. Such meetings provide an opportunity to establish something of the depth of personality of a life that is becoming more difficult to access each day. The information that is revealed in these conversations is crucial in formulating any notion of the needs of the patient or user. Each comment carries with it the potential for understanding who this person is, at a time when the much-trusted tools of understanding are slipping beyond one's grasp.

Individual histories, the narratives of our lives, move us into a spiritual dimension where the 'Who', 'Why' and 'Where' questions can be addressed. For those with dementia, answers to such questions are perhaps more urgent than ever before. In the early stages, there will be a realization that limited time is available to deal with these issues. But the development of dementia does not mean that there can no longer be any self-understanding or capacity to frame the answers. It is perhaps just that new tools are necessary.

The practice of religion, with its extensive use of ritual, symbol and non-verbal forms of communication such as silence and music, coupled with the experience of community when meeting together, offers a range of such tools. Those who might be considered likely to benefit from regular religious activity will be identified from the pastoral conversations. In turn, if the pastoral carers (the health-care staff) are communicative and the religious care givers (ordained or lay) are attentive, appropriate forms of spiritual and religious care can be moulded to meet the needs of both individuals and the group.

Defining the objectives of the project

Currently throughout the NHS, the concept of 'evidence-based practice' is being used to assess outcomes against previously defined aims, as a means of driving up standards. This is not a procedure that is widely utilized within the local church context, perhaps because there is an understandable aversion to the application of techniques that originate in models of organizational management to matters of God. Nonetheless, it must surely be appropriate in any religious activity, whether human or divine or a combination of the two, for there to be a means of asking whether an enterprise is of value to the participants and of worth to God.

The objectives of one spiritual or religious activity will not be the same as any other. There may well be common factors, but varieties in location, context, personnel and the like will make each set of aims unique. The three that were considered most important to the Candlelight Group (though not necessarily pre-eminent in all contexts) were as follows:

1 Coming together as a group
During the course of any week, a variety of groups will be available to service users. The very act of gathering together is a way of maintaining social contact. Although encounters with the realm of the divine can of

course occur at any time, in most faith traditions formal acts of corporate worship require a gathering of more than one. By naming the group, it was hoped that those who attended regularly would develop a sense of identity associated with the group, in a similar way to that engendered by association with or membership of a particular church.

2 Worshipping as a community

To those involved in the original discussions, a distinction was drawn between the activity of worship and the nature and aims of therapeutic or occupational groups. Worshipping as a group may have an ameliorative aspect, but this is not its primary aim. Rather, it was hoped that those who were identified as possessing a faith would meet, not so much as a 'group' but more as a 'community', displaying and developing common values, interests and a culture through the regularity and consistency of contact.

3 Thinking beyond the immediate

A reduction in the accessible timescale is one of the most readily identifiable characteristics of dementia. Short-term memory loss (albeit sometimes accompanied by a fragmented remembrance of events and personalities from much earlier periods in life), together with a reduced sense of meaning of the future, lead to a life that is increasingly lived in the here and now. By replicating each week the rhythm of the Christian year, re-telling the Christian story and sharing well-known elements of Christian worship, it was hoped that narrow perspectives of time might broaden, and a deeper sense of the individual's place in a wider universe might gradually be re-experienced.

Measuring effectiveness

Measuring outcomes against the original aims can be undertaken in many ways – observation of the time together, talking with the participants, reflecting on one's own feelings, all will offer the opportunity to assess the value of the religious encounter. Experience of the Candlelight Group suggests that the following techniques provide ways of understanding some of the psychological and religious dynamics within the group and the ways in which these might be received and understood by the participants. By understanding these, a realistic attempt can be made to evaluate the effectiveness of the encounters against the original aims.

1 Identifying the regularity of attendance

Living with dementia does not mean relinquishing all autonomy. Throughout the life of the Candlelight Group, clients who attend the day hospital have always been asked if they wish to attend the Group's act of worship. Some have declined from the outset, others have welcomed weekly invitations; some have begun to attend and subsequently dropped off, citing a variety of reasons. Some of these reasons belie deeper motives, which may need to be teased out in further conversation, but the refusal of any invitation has always been respected.

2 Conducting interviews
Immediately after the end of a service, it is possible to conduct a short interview with members of the participating group, exploring their cognitive and emotional reactions to the time spent together in worship. Because of the relatively stable nature of the group, it is also possible to carry out such interviews on a periodic basis, separated perhaps by some months, thus affording the opportunity to assess whether there have been changes in the experience. Because of the nature of dementia, most interviewees are only able to comment on the immediate encounter, making it important that the same questions are addressed each time to enable any nuances of response to be assessed on a like-for-like basis.

3 Observation
Because of the difficulties in verbal expression that accompany dementia, there may be a limitation on the value of personal interviews. To develop a broader picture, close observation of the group and its participants during their time together can often be very useful. However, this must be carried out in an unobtrusive manner. If the observations can be recorded by a regular leader, any rise in anxiety can be contained. Changes in the usual patterns of behaviour, brought about by the observation, must be taken into account when assessing the evidence that is obtained.

Videoing the service, which requires prior negotiation with and the consent of each member of the group, affords an opportunity to check and re-check observations which themselves are subject to the limitations of attention and the vagaries of one's memory. As with individual observation, the same issues of intrusion and consistency apply.

4 Leadership reflection
Because the emotions of individuals and groups are frequently transferred onto leaders, it is invariably worthwhile for those who conduct the act of worship to talk with those who are responsible for the care of the participants, both before and after the service. Examining one's own feelings once the service is over may tease out depths of feelings generated both by one's own experience and also projected from others. Living with dementia does not imply that emotions disappear or cannot be felt,

merely that they are more easily expressed sensually and spiritually than verbally.

Principles from the Candlelight Group

As is the case with journeys into unknown territory, the initial discussions between the nursing staff and the chaplains began rather gingerly, as if feeling the way forward and erring on the side of caution, mindful of the vulnerable nature of the potential participants. Yet these difficult conversations, covering challenging areas, proved invaluable. The health-care staff were able to identify those whom they felt would benefit from specific religious care; the chaplain was then able to construct an act of worship that might reasonably be expected to engage likely attenders, given the context in which the service was to be set. From the outset, certain principles that underpinned the worship were adopted:

1 Simplicity
Simplicity does not imply a patronizing attitude to those with dementia, although the loss of some cognitive functions and modes of verbal expression needs to be acknowledged. Often, though, the simpler the act of worship, the more effective it is. Convoluted words, obscure imagery and complicated symbolism frequently fail to engage the worshipper – and probably God as well! Primarily, it was agreed that simplicity was to be reflected in a straightforward liturgical form, the use of plain language and a powerful symbol – the candle.

2 Non-Eucharistic form
For many Christians, regular attendance at Holy Communion is the central expression of their faith. There is undoubtedly a place for this practice to be continued when it is difficult or even impossible for attendance within a faith community to be maintained; hence the widespread practice of bringing the Reserved Sacrament to home or ward. However, because of differences in theological understanding between Christian denominations, Holy Communion can turn out to be divisive and excluding. Roman Catholics may feel unable to take Communion from Anglican clergy; Roman Catholics priests may not be able to offer it to non-Catholics; and Non-conformists may feel uncomfortable with sharing a common cup.

Thus it was felt that, if group identification and unity were to be achieved and valued, a non-Eucharistic form of worship ought to be adopted as the norm. Such a decision had the added advantage that the service could be led by lay or ordained persons and could therefore be a regular fixture in the life of the day hospital, irrespective of the availability of the clergy. Indeed, with a little training and a sensitive understanding of and approach to worship, it was felt that certain health-care staff would also be equipped to lead the group.

3 Short duration

Because the concentration and attention span of the attenders was anticipated to be of limited duration, it was initially decided that the act of worship should be kept to a maximum of twenty minutes. However, as time has gone by, this has been found not to be so vital a consideration. Careful observation has revealed that, once the group is comfortable with the liturgy, they are able to engage either with individual sections or with the whole order of service. Much will depend on their own spiritual and religious needs, their emotional state at the time of the service and their general position on the spectrum of dementia, but the first two of these criteria might easily apply to all of us. As a result, the service now lasts about 30 minutes, with few instances of disruption by or discomfort for the participants.

4 Familiarity

From the outset, the format of the Candlelight Group's liturgy has been replicated each week. Even when the lead chaplain changed, the service continued in its original format. In particular, the opening hymn is always the same; the Lord's Prayer, in its original version, has a central position; the ritual lighting of candles and their use as votive symbols plus an ending with the Grace all reinforce familiarity and enable participation. As a result, after an initial period during which recognition of these elements becomes embedded, even those who have poor recollection began to recognize them and participate in the act of worship in ways that are appropriate to them personally.

Although the four principles that have just been articulated apply to the Candlelight Group in particular, it is likely that they will resonate with other settings. Discussions with primary care givers and those invited to provide spiritual and religious care may draw out other criteria that will act as foundations on which to construct the liturgical vehicle for religious encounters. But once the principles have been established, the core theology has been undertaken and the groundwork laid, the invitation to provide spiritual and religious care to those with dementia in the local residential home, day centre or hospital can be accepted. Theoretical considerations must now become practical reality.

Practical considerations

Here we identify some of the pitfalls that have been encountered (including some ideas on how to avoid them) and point to some areas where a little time spent beforehand will produce much fruit on the day.

These practicalities presuppose a level of cognition and verbal expression that enables there to be a degree of effective and mutually understandable communication. This will not always be the case. Those with significant reductions in these functions will respond to a shorter, simpler, less verbal liturgy, involving familiar symbolism. Indeed, words may play little or no part, whereas music may stimulate far more recognition. Yet, whatever the extent of the dementia, there is no theological or pastoral reason for avoiding the provision of spiritual and religious care.

The space

1 Space for gathering together
Within most care settings, it is extremely unlikely that a room can be set aside solely for religious purposes. So the choice of the room or space in which to gather for a service has to be made quite carefully. First, identify the likely numbers of participants and keep to this general number unless you have a choice of rooms.

If possible, negotiate the use of a space that is in a quiet location in the building. Battling against the exercise class is not conductive to worship! Paradoxically, a space that is very visible can often prompt those who pass it to drop their voices and respect the act of worship.

The space should be:

- small enough to retain a sense of intimacy;
- large enough for any who are disabled to manoeuvre safely;
- capable of housing armchairs to place participants at their ease.

Before selecting the room, work out the layout of the furniture, check the provision of sockets for any tape or CD player, work out the ease of access to a piano or keyboard if you wish to use one, and so on. In addition, think through any possible liturgical movements and make sure you are able to achieve these without tripping over feet or falling into participants' laps!

2 Sharing the room

Do not be concerned about sharing space that is used for another purpose.

If you are presented with a large day room, find screens or perhaps arrange some dining chairs to delineate the space you wish to use, but move them back when you have finished, so as not to inconvenience the staff.

If there are available walls, see if you are allowed to remove a picture and hang an appropriate religious symbol in its place for the duration of the service. If this is not possible, create the focal point by means of a low table, or a symbol placed on the floor, that conveys a sense of the sacred.

3 Access to and from the space

Ensure there is sufficient width of access for wheelchairs and that there are few, if any, awkward thresholds to navigate. Modern buildings should not have these problems and hazards; older, converted buildings may still contain them.

Always ensure that a trained member of staff is responsible for guiding disabled patients to and from the room and into and out of chairs. They are the experts in health care; you are the experts in spiritual care. Recognize the difference!

The liturgy

1 Service sheets

In addition to the effects of dementia, older age invariably brings with it eyesight difficulties, so:

- produce service sheets in large print (14 or 16 point should suffice) in a clear font (try Tahoma, Montreal, Gill Sans or Arial);
- provide clear headings for each section – it will aid following the service and re-finding positions if they are lost;
- introduce symbols or pictures to amplify the purpose of the text (e.g. hands together for prayers, musical notes for songs).

If the service is to be used on a regular basis, laminate the service sheets for easy cleaning.

2 Beginning and ending

Whatever form the act of worship takes, always begin and end clearly. Avoid the tendency to slide into and out of the service. It only creates uncertainty, particularly at the start, if no one is quite sure whether proceedings have commenced.

Perhaps begin with an action, such as lighting a candle or with words such as, 'We meet in the name of the Living God'.

End with a blessing, or by saying the Grace together. If you started by lighting a candle, why not end by extinguishing it?

3 Scripture

Select passages of the Bible that are focused, and keep them short. Long passages from Paul's writings or detailed lists of dietary rules from Leviticus will be difficult to follow and impossible to remember for any length of time. If there is a choice between Gospel accounts of the same events, select the simplest (Mark's Gospel is often helpful here).

If you wish to print out the reading for participants to follow:

* use large print and a clear font;
* incorporate a symbol (e.g. an open Bible) at the top of the page;
* print on coloured paper (but avoid black words on red, which are very difficult to read).

4 Hymns and songs

Hymns that were popular in the decades on either side of the Second World War are most likely to be known by those in the group. Sunday School, or its equivalent, may also be a fruitful source for songs. However, do not overlook more modern popular hymns and songs, since members of the group, from whatever tradition, might well have sung these regularly in the past 25 years.

Whatever you choose:

* keep to those with strict rhythms and regular verse patterns, so as to reduce uncertainty and hold everyone together;
* if you are singing to a CD or tape, check the recording first for introductions, descants and the general speed;
* print out the words of hymns or songs in large print and a clear font on coloured paper (but one that is different from the Bible reading), with an appropriate suitable symbol at the head of the page;
* check that the words on the sheet tally with those sung on the CD or tape; alternatively, use a music-only CD.

5 Prayer

The time of prayer offers one of the most important opportunities to explore spiritual questions around personal identity and the individual participant's relationship to God. It provides space for an expression of deep emotional and religious feelings. It is also a democratizing opportunity, when those who are less able to verbalize their feelings can express them through gesture and symbol.

Many prayer options are available – intercessory and thanksgiving forms, litanies, biddings and silence, and many more. Consider using symbols that can be held by or attributed to each participant – e.g. candles, pebbles, small crosses, etc. – but take great care to ensure that small symbols do not find their way into a mouth!

Do not underestimate the capacity of participants to name either the subjects or objects of their prayers and concerns out loud, or to pick up on the theme from the scriptures, hymns or reflections used earlier in the service.

When participants remember those who have died in war, the silence will be broken only by the sound of restrained sobbing at memories of past experiences or loved ones who never came back.

Communication

1 Liturgical colours
One of the ways of marking the passage of time throughout the Church's year is by varying the coloured cloths, which can be placed over any table that is used for liturgical purposes:

- purple for Advent and Lent, the penitential periods, the times of waiting;
- white for Christmas, Epiphany and Easter, when the mood is one of celebration;
- red for the fire of Pentecost and the blood of those saints who were martyred;
- green for the growth of Ordinary Time, between Epiphany and Ash Wednesday, and Pentecost and Advent.

Once participants have absorbed the meaning of the symbolism (which can be observed and noted right at the beginning of each service), it acts as an aid to recognition of the time in the liturgical year, which itself reflects the secular calendar.

However, ensure that, while the cloths are long enough to cover the table generously, they are not so long as to trail on the floor where they will pose a safety hazard.

2 Symbols
Symbols are an excellent way of signifying something important without the necessity for words. But choose them carefully.

Crosses are a universal Christian symbol, but those people of low churchmanship may be offended by the use of crucifixes.

Icons are from a specific tradition but offer a meditative way into the major events and characters of the Christian narrative.

Candles are very popular, but:

- place them in such a way that they cannot be touched inadvertently;
- do not allow participants to hold them or place their service sheets on top of them;
- extinguish them before participants move around the room.

3 Interaction

Within some traditions of Christian worship, direct interaction between the leader and the participants can be rare. Usually, boundaries are clear; leaders lead and congregations follow. We sit or kneel for prayer and stand up and sing when hymns or songs are announced. We listen attentively when scripture is being read, concentrate hard when the sermon is preached (don't we?) and repeat credal statements together as a unifying act. It is not exactly Pavlovian, but if someone says, 'Let us pray', do we not automatically drop to our knees or sit down?

One of the liberating things about dementia is that these well-erected and pretty firm boundaries become very much more pliable. Comments are sometimes made at moments that appear inappropriate or discon-nected, and questions are asked when something is not clear. Because the conventions of worship, established for the sake of good order, are more lightly held, interaction becomes not only a reality but often the life-blood of the religious encounter.

Within the encounter, it is important to speak clearly and distinctly. Age tends to reduce the quality of hearing, and the effects of dementia adversely affect the memory, so the understanding of verbal instructions (such as requests for prayer) or the impact of scripture readings is dependent on the ability of the participants to identify and hold key words and phrases. It is therefore important to speak clearly and distinctly and to frame phrases or questions in a straightforward manner.

Where music is concerned, keep the volume up fairly loud, so as to give a firm lead.

However, do not be afraid of silence. It may be interrupted, but if you have signalled it by instruction, symbol or a clear liturgical gesture, there is little reason to suppose that it will not be observed. Indeed, at times such as the National Remembrance or All Souls-tide, the silence is invari-ably total and very moving.

If there are blind or visually impaired participants present, do not forget to address them directly and describe any symbols or actions as you proceed through the service.

4 *Changing direction*

One of the consequences of interaction that is most frequently encountered is the challenge to be prepared to change direction from that which was lovingly thought out and prepared beforehand. The 'Encounter and Reflection' section of the Candlelight Group service is deliberately loosely framed to encourage interaction. Whoever leads it has a sense of the direction in which it is intended to go and the point at which it should conclude.

But the flexibility of the boundaries is deliberately intended to allow the direction of the encounter to be varied according to participants' contributions. Sometimes, an interjection may not appear to have any connection with that which immediately precedes it. But to disregard it is to make a value judgement about the validity of one's own thought processes against those of another's. At the very least, the contribution must be acknowledged and taken seriously. At best, it will offer a new path of exploration that may lead the group rather unexpectedly into the heart of God.

5 *Working in pairs*

Engaging in pastoral, spiritual and religious care with those with dementia presents a wonderful opportunity to empower others. There are so many people in faith communities, of all ages, who possess the compassion and latent skills to engage in this form of care. Yet they are often reticent to come forward and are thus frequently overlooked. Similarly, nursing staff and care assistants invariably shy away from getting involved in what is seen as the chaplain's area of expertise.

Working in pairs in delivering these forms of care has great advantages. At the point of gathering, a doorkeeper can act as a welcomer, while another can help participants to find a seat. During the service, one can deal with any issues of discomfort or distress, leaving the worship leader free to hold things together for the benefit of the rest of the group.

However, during a period of reflection, both can participate, each picking up on the flow of conversation and the individual comments that are made. The more personal experiences can be utilized in this part of the service, the more effective it will be as a vehicle for a spiritual encounter with the divine.

And at the end, there is the opportunity of sharing the experience and personal observations of time spent together in the presence of God and each other.

Applications to other faiths

The Candlelight Group was developed to provide an act of worship for Christians and this short chapter is unapologetically applicable to this faith group. Yet behind it, particularly in the NHS, lies a multi-faith agenda. In many major towns, an ethnically diverse population almost inevitably implies that facilities such as residential care homes, psycho-geriatric wards and day hospitals for older people will contain a culturally diverse mix of persons. This is both a daunting challenge and a rich resource.

It is a mistake to assume that what works for Christians is transferable to the context of other faiths. Pastoral, spiritual and religious care is inter-preted in very different ways by other faith groups. Theology, culture and ethnicity all ask questions around spiritual and religious care that will lead to fundamentally different answers depending on the faith con-cerned. Yet to assume that multi-faith religious care is an impossibility is to give up before the first hurdle.

Just as Christianity is not a monolithic religion, neither are other faiths. It is perhaps as true to say that conservative evangelical Christians have little common theological language with their Anglo-Catholic 'brethren' as it is to say that Sunni, Shia and Sufi Muslims will not find complete religious unanimity with each other. The roots of the tree may be the same, but the subsequent branch patterns are invariably very different.

Multi-faith engagement in the United Kingdom often tends to be reductionist in content. The liturgical elements of multi-faith gatherings are primarily designed not to offend rather than to affirm. They invari-ably seek the lowest common denominator on which different groups can agree, rather than celebrating difference within a theological framework of exploration. The validity of either approach needs to be considered carefully and critically with authorized representatives of other faiths before embarking on any multi-faith project.

Some faith groups, such as the Jewish community, already have in place effective programmes of religious care, since there is a longstanding culture of general health care for older people within the faith. Dialogue with those responsible for the delivery of such programmes provides an effective starting point. Whatever the perceived call for spiritual and religious care of those with dementia might be across the spectrum of cultures, the majority faith must be very careful to avoid any charge of religious imperialism. A dialogue of equals, exploring differences in approach, would seem to be a fruitful starting point.

SECTION 4

A Good Death for People with Dementia

Chapter 9

End-of-life Care for People with Dementia

KATHERINE FROGGATT

We all fear death. In particular, those older people who have had time to contemplate their mortality may wonder what shape death may take for them and whether it will be pain free. In 2003 Katherine Froggatt studied end-of-life care in care homes in Australia and Canada as a Sir Winston Churchill Fellow. She brings some of this learning to a reflection on the difficulties involved in applying the concept of palliative care or end-of-life care to people living with dementia, who may have limited awareness of what is happening and for whom the dying process may extend over several years.

Introduction

End-of-life care for people with dementia is a complex area that challenges us as a society and as individuals. This chapter aims to give an overview of end-of-life care for people with dementia, through a consideration of both policy and practice initiatives which influence the care provision for people dying with dementia and their families. Knowledge of the broader policy context within which care provision is delivered sets the scene. This is contrasted with different roles played by the individuals directly affected by the end-of-life transitions of people with dementia. Palliative care specializes in the care of people who are dying from terminal illnesses other than dementia, so the relevance of palliative care for people with dementia is discussed. Finally, challenges present in the provision of care towards the end of life for people with dementia are presented.

Background

Dementia is present, in some form, in many people's lives in the United Kingdom. This is especially so for older people. It is estimated that 25 per cent of people over 65 years old live with dementia.[1] Other people in the population affected by dementia include people who live with someone with dementia, care for someone with dementia, either as family carers, professional carers or volunteers, and a wider group of people who may not be directly involved in care but know individuals and their families living with this condition.

Those people whom dementia affects are also likely to have to engage ultimately with dying and death. The median length of survival from diagnosis of dementia to death is estimated to be eight years.[2] While this is a longer period than for some other conditions, dementia remains associated with death, especially among older people. For the purpose of this chapter, 'end-of-life' refers to any period of time towards the end of a person's life that can be identified, at least with hindsight, as leading to their death. For people with dementia, this may mean months or years. End-of-life may be less clearly identifiable than with other terminal conditions such as cancer, which have a more predictable and shorter pattern of progression.

The United Kingdom policy context

Within the United Kingdom, a range of policy initiatives has been introduced in recent years that promotes particular understandings of the ageing process and how this should be managed. These policy initiatives bring an emphasis on choice, independence and health, as identified in *Building on the Best*.[3] Within the care for older people field, rehabilitation and intermediate care for older people is encouraged in the *National Service Framework for Older People*[4] and the *Care Homes for Older People: National Minimum Standards*.[5] More specific initiatives in palliative care, for example the NICE *Guidance on Cancer Services: Improving Supportive and Palliative Care for People with Cancer*[6] and the *End-of-life Initiative*[7] also stress elements of choice and provision of care in a person's own home as being a priority.

It is interesting to note that the older-people policy initiatives contain only a limited focus on end-of-life care, and therefore the extent to which end-of-life issues can be fully addressed may be questioned. The placing of people with dementia in policy initiatives concerned with older people rather than long-term neurological conditions also has implications for the specific needs of younger people with dementia. Their needs may not be adequately met because of this.

The individual perspective

Understanding the issues of dying with dementia can also be considered from a number of different individual perspectives. Three are described here: the individuals with dementia, family members of the person with dementia who are sometimes also carers, and formal carers in health or social care. While I consider these different groups of people separately, it is recognized that they are interrelated and share common attributes.

The person with dementia

People with dementia are not a homogeneous group. They are a diverse group of people with different demographic, social and illness characteristics that shape their experiences of living and dying with dementia.[8] As already indicated, the age of people with dementia can vary, and while the majority develop dementia in old age, there is a group of younger people who experience the onset of the illness earlier in their lives. Dementia as an illness is also not a unitary experience. People may have one of several types of dementia, each with its own manifestations and patterns, that further vary according to how advanced the disease is. Moreover, older people with dementia may also live with a number of other chronic or even acute conditions that also impact greatly upon their lives and may interact with the dementia. People's cultural and social background varies, and understandings of dementia may vary between different cultural and ethnic groups. The availability of social support from family and friends will influence an individual's experience of their illness, and this is also linked to their place of residence. An individual living in his or her own home may experience life and their illness differently from someone who lives in a care home.

Overlaying the diversity of experience of dementia is diversity in the experience of dying. Cox and Cook[9] have developed three scenarios to conceptualize dying with dementia. First, people with dementia whose death can be attributed to a medical condition that is not related to the dementia. This might include a person with mild dementia who develops cancer and then dies from cancer. Second, people with dementia may die with a complex mix of mental and physical problems where dementia is not the primary cause of death but interacts with the other conditions. Third, people with dementia may die from complications arising from end-stage dementia.

There are limitations to what we know about people's experience of dying with dementia. There is some information available from family carers who have provided a retrospective view of the dying and death of their relative. While there are obvious limitations to these accounts, in that they are proxy accounts and obtained after the event, they do provide some insight into what this period of time is like for the individual with dementia. Family carers describe a wide range of physical and psychological symptoms in the person with dementia observed by the relative. They include mental confusion, pain, urinary incontinence, low mood, constipation, loss of appetite, shortness of breath, pyrexia.[10] A perspective on people with dementia can come from people earlier on in their illness. It is understandably a difficult issue to be faced. As one person put it: 'I cannot live with all of my future life filling today's space. This would be way too heavy a load, and most likely destructive'.[11]

Family carers

The family of the person with dementia is also a diverse group with differences arising from their demographic and social status as well as each family's particular characteristics. One variation is in the age of the family members. Sometimes family carers are the same generation as the person with dementia (spouses, partners or siblings), sometimes the next generation down (children, nephews and nieces), or sometimes, for younger people with dementia, the carer may be a parent. Some family carers may also be living with their own particular health conditions that impact on their ability to care. They may also have to juggle other carer demands from different generations of the family such as young children.

The caring role may be shaped by the geographical distance from the person with dementia. The care given by a family member may be primary care (undertaking directly personal care tasks), or secondary care (visiting and supporting other family members doing the primary care). The caring roles adopted by different family members are affected by the emotional distance and type of relationships between family members; the dynamics may not be harmonious in relation to the person with dementia or within the wider family. The complexity of family life with divorce, deaths, remarriages, stepchildren and half siblings can mean that the negotiation around caring roles in the family is not always straightforward.

The experience of family carers of people with dementia has been well documented,[12] but knowledge about the end-of-life period is more limited. An American study that talked with family carers of people with moderate to severe dementia about their decision-making identified a number of issues for the family carer. Decisions were made in the context of an extended period of emotional burden and guilt. Also the changes in condition of their relative were not generally recognized as being part of a trajectory of dying which therefore impacted on the types of decisions they made. Death when it came was seen as both a tragedy and a blessing.[13]

Professional or formal carers

However much or little care individual family members give to the person with dementia at the end of life, professional carers will be involved to different degrees. There is much diversity within this group, particularly in terms of their background in care. Depending upon the place of residence of the person with dementia, he or she may receive care from people with a health-care or with a social care background. Then again, these professionals may have a general care role or be specialists in dementia care or perhaps in palliative care.

The experience of these professionals in caring for people with dementia is similarly not well documented. Care work with older people is under-valued and is under-resourced in the care home sector.[14] In palliative care, the demands on staff caring for people who are dying are recognized.[15] There is a potential for conflict between different care goals in the care for older people with dementia. Different professionals may work to different agendas: some seek a cure, others may focus on maximizing the potential of the 'patient' through rehabilitation, and others prefer to emphasize the palliation of symptoms, whether they be physical or behavioural. Careful communication and negotiation of these different approaches is required if the best interests of the person with dementia are to be met.

Care for people dying with dementia

In order to consider care provision for people dying with dementia, it is helpful to look at the distinct discipline of palliative care which has as its focus the care of people diagnosed with life-limiting illnesses such as cancer. Palliative care has its origins in the hospice movement, of which the modern manifestations began in the 1950s with Dame Cicely Saunders' establishment of St Christopher's Hospice in south London. This modern speciality has expanded from in-patient care to supporting people in hospitals, in their own homes and in care homes. It is currently diversifying to address the needs of people suffering not only from cancer but from a range of other life-limiting illnesses including neurological, respiratory and cardiac conditions – and now dementia. The goal of palliative care is defined as the achievement of the best quality of life for older people and families. This is delivered in a number of ways through the active holistic care of people with advanced, progressive illness, the management of pain and other symptoms, and the provision of psychological, social and spiritual support.[16]

Palliative care is divided into specialist and generalist provision. Specialist palliative care is provided by specialist palliative care professionals to meet complex needs (symptoms, psychosocial, bereavement) of people in all settings. Generalist palliative care is provided by generalist professionals to meet ongoing needs in all settings, but they may call upon specialist services to meet specific needs through consultancy services.

Another term increasingly used within the United Kingdom is 'end-of-life' care, although different understandings are attributed to this term. It may refer to the last few days and hours of life, or even the last few months of life, when an individual is known to be dying within a time period. Alternatively, it could be used to refer to a longer-term transition over a period of years. In Canada, the following definition is used to describe end-of-life care: '. . . an active, compassionate approach that treats, comforts and supports older adults who are living, or dying from, a progressive or chronic life threatening condition'.[17]

This definition captures the notion of a longer-term transition that incorporates a movement from life to death. For people dying with dementia, a number of elements of this transition can be identified that require attention if we are to ensure appropriate care for people at this time in their lives. Three aspects are described here: living and losses, dying and death, and bereavement.[18]

Living and losses

The onset of dementia leads to experiences of loss for the person with dementia, and their family and friends around them. An older person without dementia potentially faces a series of physical, social and emotional losses associated with an ageing body and changes that affect its ability to function as it used to. There may also be social and relational changes as family and friends themselves grow up, move away and even die. However, the person with dementia is likely to face further losses not only related to their ultimate physical death, but also associated with a social death as a person in the social world they inhabit.[19] Increased need for care may increase the likelihood that a person with dementia will need to move into a care home in the later stages of the illness. The move into a care home is an important one. How this is managed sets a precedent for the relationships established and the way in which future changes are handled. The losses associated with entry to a care home for an individual can include a move out of their own home, separation from a partner or spouse, the loss of nearby friends and neighbours and even an animal companion.

People's experiences of living in care homes are mixed. Where it is a positive experience, good relationships can be established between the person with dementia, their family members and the staff in the care home. It is experienced as a safe place in which to be. The length of time many residents live in a care home before they die creates the potential for establishing good relationships between care staff, residents and their families that is helpful when decisions are required about care choices.

Dying and death

As indicated above, there are a number of different ways in which the person with dementia may die.[20] The dying process experienced by many residents within care homes is very different from that experienced by patients cared for within a specialist palliative care context. The dying process for people with dementia is often uncertain – it is not always easy to determine when a person is actually near to death.

This raises particular concerns around decision-making with regard to end-of-life issues. The increasing difficulties in communication experienced by people with dementia mean that work around decision-making that involves the person with dementia will have to be attended to much earlier in a person's illness journey than with some other conditions. While family members can act as proxies for their relative, in some families it may not be a straightforward option as there may be a lack of clarity about who is responsible.

Also associated with the time period around the dying and death is a need to make a place for meaning-making and closure around a person's life. For a person with dementia, their active involvement in their dying may require earlier attention – before an individual is 'known' to be dying. Meaning-making may address spiritual needs and, especially in later stages, may draw on non-verbal activities and make use of symbol or familiar rituals.

Bereavement(s)

While the person with dementia will be experiencing the bereavement that arises from their own forthcoming death, it is family members who are faced with the ongoing bereavement because the person they know and love is slowly deteriorating and losing physical and cognitive function over a long period of time.[21] So, too, professional carers may be facing bereavement as the person dies, but maybe with less legitimate space to acknowledge this.

Challenges around dying with dementia

From the issues laid out in this chapter, a number of challenges can be identified in relation to seeking to meet the needs of people dying with dementia. First, there is a challenge to hold both living and dying together, not one at the expense of the other. An emphasis on healthy ageing and maximizing the potential of older people may be helpful in many situations, at particular points in time. However, if we do not allow space for increasing frailty, infirmity and even death, which is the inevitable end-point of ageing, then it becomes unhelpful. To go to the other extreme of immediately associating a diagnosis of dementia with dying does not allow for the living that can still be experienced, and is equally unhelpful. We need to find ways of holding on to both living and dying.

Working with people living and dying with dementia occurs over a longer time-frame than usually encountered in palliative care work. The needs of people with dementia may require us to undertake sensitive preparatory work earlier on in a person's illness than is normally done with other conditions such as cancer. If we are to honour and value the person with dementia, then we need to find ways in which people with dementia, family members, professionals and volunteers can work with these difficult issues, at times when they are able and willing to do so. It is difficult to involve people with dementia in these processes early on in their illness, when death is not imminent, but the communication challenges present later on in the illness mean that this time is an important one. When verbal communication is less easy, other forms of non-verbal or symbolic communication need to be found.

Finally, there is the challenge of working within and beyond the current system of resources. The financial resources for care, staffing and environments of care are unlikely to increase significantly in the near future. We need to seek imaginative ways to address needs both inside and beyond the existing systems of care. We should value, and seek to make our systems value, people with dementia as they live and die with this illness.

Acknowledgements

I would like to acknowledge my colleagues Professor Murna Downs and Professor Neil Small at the University of Bradford for the ongoing discussions that have helped form these ideas.

Notes

1 Hofman, A., Rocca, W., Brayne, C., Breteler, M., Clarke, M., Cooper, B., Copeland, J., Dartigues, J., da Silva Droux, A. and Hagnell, O., 'The Prevalence of Dementia in Europe: A Collaborative Study of 1980–1990 Findings', Eurodem Prevalence Research Group, *International Journal of Epidemiology*, 20, 1991, pp. 736–48.

2 Ibid.

3 Department of Health, *Building on the Best: Choice, Responsiveness and Equity in the NHS*, HMSO, 1993).

4 Department of Health, *National Service Framework for Older People*, 2001.

5 Department of Health, *Care Homes for Older People: National Minimum Standards*, HMSO, 2003.

6 National Institute for Clinical Excellence, *Guidance on Cancer Services: Improving Supportive and Palliative Care for People with Cancer*, 2004.

7 Department of Health, Press Notice, 26 December 2003.

8 Cox, S. and Cook, A., 'Caring for People with Dementia at the End of Life' in Hockley, J. and Clark, D. (eds), *Palliative Care for Older People in Care Homes*, Open University Press, 2002, pp. 86–103.

9 Ibid.

10 Lloyd-Williams, M., 'An Audit of Palliative Care in Dementia', *European Journal of Cancer Care*, 5, 1996, pp. 53–5; McCarthy, M., Addington-Hall, J. and Altmann, D., 'The Experience of Dying with Dementia: A Retrospective Study', *International Journal of Geriatric Psychiatry*, 12, 1997, pp. 404–9.

11 Raushi, T., 'Something Was Not Right' in Doka, K. (ed), *Living with Grief Alzheimer's Disease*, Hospice Foundation of America, 2004, pp. 99–109.

12 Marriott, A., 'Helping Families Cope with Dementia' in Adams, T. and Manthorpe, J. (eds), *Dementia Care*, Arnold, 2003, pp. 187–201.

13 Forbes, S., Bern-Klug, M. and Gessert, C., 'End-of-life Decision Making for Nursing Home Residents with Dementia', *Journal of Nursing Scholarship*, 32 (3), 2000, pp. 251–8.

14 Davies, S. and Seymour, J., 'Historical and Policy Contexts' in Hockley, J. and Clark, D. (eds), *Palliative Care for Older People in Care Homes*, Open University Press, 2002, pp. 4–33.

15 Aranda, S., 'The Cost of Caring' in Payne, S., Seymour, J. and Ingleton, C. (eds), *Palliative Care Nursing*, Open University Press, 2004, pp.620–34.

16 National Institute for Clinical Excellence, *Guidance on Cancer Services: Improving Supportive and Palliative Care for People with Cancer*, 2004.

17 Ross, M., Fisher, R. and MacLean, M., *A Guide to End-of-Life Care for Seniors*, Health Canada, 2000.

18 Froggatt, K., *Palliative Care in Care Homes for Older People*, The National Council for Palliative Care, 2004.

19 Sweeting, H. and Gilhooly, M., 'Dementia and the Phenomenon of Social Death', *Sociology of Health and Illness*, 19 (1), 1997, pp. 93–117.

20 Cox, S. and Cook, A., 2002, op. cit., pp. 86–103.

21 Seymour, J., Witherspoon, R., Gott, M., Ross, H., Payne, S. and Owen, T., *End of Life Care: Promoting Comfort, Choice and Well Being for Older People at the End of Their Lives*, The Policy Press with Help the Aged, 2005.

Chapter 10

The Terminal Care of People with Dementia at Home

ADRIAN TRELOAR

Dr Adrian Treloar is a senior lecturer and consultant in old-age psychiatry and a committed Christian. He brings his faith to bear upon the issues of choice and end-of-life care. He shows us how the option of continuing to care for a person with dementia at home until the end is both desirable and practicable. He offers case studies where it has been done successfully and explores the conditions which are required to make it possible. One of the notable lessons of this chapter is that systems of care need to be more flexible and responsive to the individual. Our approach to care would look very different if we shared Adrian Treloar's imaginative compassion and insight.

Case examples

Grace, in her seventies, developed a multi-infarct dementia. She became very agitated and distressed, and went into a nursing home. Within two weeks she had lost weight, was bruised, distressed and ended up sitting on a dementia assessment ward. Sitting in a basket chair, she called out repeatedly numbers from 97 to 100. It was difficult to see what could be done to alleviate her distress or to care for her. Judicious use of anti-psychotics and antidepressants had some benefit, and benzodiazepines were used as well. She didn't do all that well but settled enough to go into a dementia specialist nursing home. There she continued to lose weight and to be distressed, and her husband could not bear to see her in such a way. He asked if he could take her home. The nurses and consultant all said they were very worried about this and thought it a bad idea. Her husband insisted, and after discussion it was agreed that this could be tried. Wonderfully, Grace did well. In fact she lived at home for eight years. She gained weight and was happy in the care of her husband along with a small but loyal group of carers who supported her husband. For a lady who was fully dependent and needed full nursing care including feeding, it was extraordinary to see her on trips out to shopping centres and her beloved golf club. Grace's long survival was, I think, attributable to the combination of good care with the fact that this was a multi-infarct dementia and not an Alzheimer's type dementia. Her dementia stabilized for quite some time and did not progress, explaining the unusually long length of time at home.

Others caring for those with dementia have had similar experiences, keeping their loved ones at home for between a couple of months and two to three years. Some went home from nursing homes. Overall, we have looked after fifteen or so patients with such needs at home over the past five years in Bexley and Greenwich. With no dedicated funding and no formal service, we are currently caring for eight such people in their homes.

One lady, surrounded by family in prayer, had not responded for 48 hours to anything. She made a sign of the cross: the last sign of responsiveness she made in her life. She died peacefully that night. It felt almost inconceivable that the opportunity of family presence in such a way could have been achieved elsewhere.

Introduction

Very many people have the aspiration that when they die, they will die at home in the care of their loved ones. Of course this is not achieved in reality for all those who aspire to it. In cancer care, large efforts have been made to develop community teams who will provide palliative care and advice on all aspects that patients need in order to stay at home. This work has been successful and well received by local communities and funded by charitable money.

By contrast, the vast majority of people with dementia die in hospital or residential/nursing care. Few people with advanced and complex dementia die at home, and few live at home in the months or years leading up to the end of their life. In part, this may be because the demands of advanced dementia are not the same as the demands of cancer care. Increased levels of agitation, depression, psychoses and behaviour disturbance are all common features of severe dementia. The fact that people with severe dementia have poor mental capacity and poor understanding is an additional cause of complexity. Often enough, palliative care in other situations can be implemented at a time when the patient is mentally competent and able to understand and work with the things that are being proposed and done for them.

Despite these problems, it is now clear that care for advanced dementia at home is feasible. Experience in south-east London has shown that regular input at home, with specialist medical and nursing advice and support, has enabled people with advanced dementia, requiring 24-hour nursing and physical care, to be provided for at home up until the time of their death. Early results from qualitative research have shown that things were better as a result of care at home and that the success of such care requires a broad range of categories of support to make it successful.

Intrinsic carer factors

We think that it is necessary for carers to be relatively robust, determined to succeed and in reasonable physical and mental health. Mental frailty in the key carer seems to be particularly problematic. The key carer will often be a spouse, but at other times may be a daughter or son or a friend. We have found that carers face obstructions in the work they do and at times have had to negotiate robustly with care managers, doctors, nurses and others. Many carers have had to purchase equipment which they found they could not get soon enough from statutory services. While in one sense at least this is quite unacceptable, it does seem to reflect the reality that this style of care is not well facilitated by statutory services. Each carer, however robust, requires the support of others.

Appliances

A wide range of appliances is needed. Hospital beds which can be raised and lowered and adjusted are almost universally required. Cushions which will raise pillows effectively are important and often not provided. Zimmer frames, commodes, bath seats, wheelchairs, showers (or better, wet rooms) and many other bits of equipment should be available when needed. Proper pressure-relieving cushions for chairs are also needed.

Later on, hoists are required. Standing hoists (when the patient is suspended from a single point) are obtainable from primary care trusts, but many of our patients have also needed sitting hoists. So when hoists are needed for care at home, they have to be available on time: if the carer can no longer lift their loved one, they will end up in care as a result. Carpet-cleaners help too!

Space and people power

Some patients have been cared for in large Victorian homes with large families and lots of people. Others have been cared for in one-bedroom maisonettes and small cottages. It is therefore possible to provide this style of care in a wide range of settings. An important principle is the willingness to alter the furniture of any setting. Space must be made to meet the primary need of bed, space for personal care, hoists and all the other bits of equipment required. Space for people to sit around a bed is also very useful. Sometimes the happiest moments for patients appear to be when two or three people are gathered around a bed where the patient can rest and where conversation about ordinary and normal things can continue.

Obstructions

Reluctant care managers, funding disputes, uncertainty about whether a person resides in the district where they own their home or with the family with whom they are staying, and many other factors have led to apparent obstruction to the provision of care at home. Often enough it may be that care managers, doctors and nurses are fearful that patients will come to harm as a result of being cared for at home. And yet dementia is a terminal illness: surely in such a circumstance it is right to take some risks to put in place a care structure that persons closest believe will make the quality of life better.

Care workers

Care workers' rotas and working out what carers will do is crucial. It has been found that when carers are commissioned by statutory authorities there are sometimes problems with flexibility. A care plan gets written and care workers may be reluctant to work outside of that care plan or to vary what they do according to what is needed. Many of our carers have found that it is important to be substantially in control of the commissioning and designing of the care plan covering what gets done. This has been variously achieved by directly employing care workers and also it can be helped by direct payments. With direct payments the key carer is given money which they can spend themselves and directly to employ care workers. It certainly is the case, for example, that if someone has just been to the toilet, and a care worker then turns up with toileting on the care plan, then it is unnecessary to toilet the person again. Rather, other appropriate tasks should be substituted. Sadly, it is often the case that if toileting is declined, care workers will leave without having done anything else.

Hospital and respite care

This is needed in some circumstances and sometimes is appropriate.

Money

The cost of doing this has been between £50 and £850 per week. We have once seen a package which cost more than £2,000 a week, but again in this circumstance there were thought to be considerable benefits for a patient who was not otherwise manageable in a continuing care setting. Certainly the weekly cost of care at home is, for the majority of people, lower than nursing home care. That the quality of life is better is perhaps a more compelling reason for promoting care at home. It is, however, heartening to know that such styles of care do not, generally, provide an additional cost pressure upon local health and social services.

Direct payments are useful. Continuing care money from primary care trusts should be available for complex management of dementia at home and has been provided for quite a number of patients.

Medication

Opiate analgesia is needed for some patients. It is not, however, frequently used and does not appear to be a mainstay of the management of advanced dementia. Anti-depressants are frequently used: there is a very high rate of depression in patients with dementia. Anti-psychotics are also important. The high frequency of psychosis in dementia, as well as the fact that behaviour problems in dementia are often driven by a psychosis which cannot be otherwise expressed, should not be forgotten. The evidence base that distress and behaviour disturbance for some people with dementia responded to anti-psychotics is strong. These drugs do, however, cause side-effects (including stroke): the question therefore is whether or not the risk of side-effects outweighs the benefit accrued by effectively relieving the torment suffered by the patient. In a palliative care setting it must be acceptable to use drugs that can harm to alleviate severe distress which cannot otherwise be managed.

Antibiotics are important in some circumstances. Some antibiotics such as erythromycin and ampicillin are unpalatable and require larger volumes of liquid for about twenty doses. Others such as azithromycin only require four to six doses of low-volume medicine. This can be a real asset to dementia care when the patient is reluctant to take medicines. Similarly antidepressants and anti-psychotics which dissolve on the tongue can be very helpful. At times medicines may be put in foodstuffs.[1] Anti-dementia drugs do not seem to be particularly useful. Memantine may help some of the behaviour disturbance.

Food and diet

Good food, nicely presented regularly and often, cut up into small pieces, is helpful. Dogged persistence is also important: it may take a while for carers to get the hang of dietary support. A number of carers have found some particular 'secret weapons'. Guava juice is high in calories and it doesn't seem to be acidic. Thickened soups, peanut butter sandwiches and chocolate baby foods have all been found by some carers to be particularly helpful.

One particularly important point is to remember that people with advanced dementia often seem to have days when they don't particularly want to eat. Carers can be very worried about this: we often think that if someone does not eat three meals a day they are getting ill. We have found that if the patient does not want to eat and cannot be encouraged to do so without conflict and stress, it is often best just to leave them be. If they don't eat one day, they will often need a bit more the next day. Taking this approach may cause some trepidation because carers may feel they will die quicker from poor nutrition. In fact, we have generally found it is not the case. Patients have lived a considerable length of time after this approach has been taken.

Spiritual support

Perhaps the greatest spiritual need for patients is to feel loved and cared for by those whom they know and whom they value. Time spent sitting with a patient is important. It is essential to remember that no response from the patient does not mean that what has been said or done has not been felt. Many people who recover from episodes when they could not respond can recall and retell what was said and happened with surprising accuracy. We have seen patients very close to death suddenly show evidence that they are aware (perhaps by making a sign of the cross or saying prayers) and other patients suddenly come out with lucid comments at times when they were not thought to be aware or hearing. The mere fact of being with someone having conversations with those around about day-to-day things is important and very positive for those with advanced dementia. Doing things at times of interaction is also important. Many people are not good at sitting doing and saying nothing. Feeding, personal care where possible, and other activities are good things therefore for carers to do with their loved ones. Set prayers, reading from religious texts and so on may be helpful. Specific prayers appropriate for those who are dying may also be helpful – see http://www.catholicdoctors.org.uk/Miscellaneous/Prayers_for_the_dying.pdf.

The need for specialist teams

We think that the complexities around the managing of complex and advanced dementia at home require a special approach. It is widely accepted that the Macmillan style approach of community teams supporting patients at home with cancer is right. Even though the components of care provided by Macmillan teams can normally be provided by others within their knowledge and competence base, it is well accepted that a specialist team does better. We believe that the same applies for dementia care. The challenges of managing complex and advanced dementia at home are significantly different from cancer care, but the principle that a specialist team should co-ordinate services and the professionals is completely valid. We hope very much that we will see the creation of such teams and research into their effectiveness in the near future. A professional who is known to the patient and carer, and who will visit and monitor proactively, has been strongly identified as a requirement by our research. Reactive visiting by primary care staff and others at times of crisis is simply inadequate.

Conclusions

If it can be done, the terminal care of dementia at home is a good idea. It appears to be, in some cases, a better way for the patient. Dying people can continue to provide benefits for those around them up to the moment of death. Perhaps at home with the family, death is more human. Perhaps also bereavement is easier to handle.

Terminal care of dementia at home is not suitable for all, and should not be considered as the only way. Residential and nursing care is needed for many people, and there are times during an illness when people will require a different sort of care. We believe that care at home requires specialist teams, although at the present time many are having to do it without any support of a co-ordinated nature.

Note

1   Treloar, A., Philpot, M. and Beats, B., 'Concealing Medication in Patients' Food', *Lancet*, 357, 2001, pp. 62–4.

Chapter 11

Meeting the Needs of a Person with Dementia in a Care Home

MARGARET GOODALL

Margaret Goodall is a Methodist minister with long experience of working with older people, and especially those living with dementia. In this compre-hensive chapter she looks at 'the long goodbye' of people in the last stages of dementia in the context of the care home. She suggests that the search for meaning is the overriding spiritual need of people living with dementia as they approach the end of life. The chapter grounds what we share when we talk about the 'spiritual dimension'.

Those coming to live in residential homes wish for 'a home for life'. With this comes the need for special care for those at the end of their life. For those with dementia this can be weeks, months or even years when it seems that the person has gone and we are waiting for the body to catch up. But taking the time to affirm the person as someone of value changes our approach to them and we see the person, not a job to be done.

Staff in care homes are asked to assess the person's physical, emotional and spiritual needs. Physical needs can be straightforward and solutions can be offered to make the person comfortable. Emotional needs can be met through socializing and personal contact. But spiritual needs can be a puzzle unless we know of faith or church affiliation.

Neglect of the spiritual dimension

In their 1971 report, the World Assembly on Ageing, sponsored by the United Nations, concluded that neglect of the spiritual dimension seriously impoverishes life and that confusional states may be greatly exacerbated by such neglect.

From working alongside care staff I have found that when there is awareness of spiritual needs, then the care reaches another level and can enable a good death for the person with dementia and their loved ones, so that they are able to affirm these words: 'I have fought the good fight, I have run the race. I have kept the faith' (2 Timothy 4.7).

Recently I have been involved in reviewing care plans for residents: there seemed to be problems with the page entitled 'Spiritual Care'. I was asked what else they could put, as the same thing seemed to be written each time; for example, 'attends church service'. Spiritual well-being does not only have to be evidenced in religious practice, but may arise from an awareness of meaning and purpose in life.

I am often asked why we bother, because it could be that to offer care to those with dementia is a waste of valuable resources on those who are not able to respond and who would not benefit. I am aware too that a great deal is expected of care staff and that they need support in order to be able to deliver the quality of care that we expect.

Spiritual needs of a dying person from a Christian perspective

There are some general 'needs' that may help us to offer spiritual care:

- The need for a God who is present. This is a God who loves and cares about the person and whose compassion can be imagined through images such as lying in the hand of God rather than in a bed, or talking with God under an oak tree in a green pasture, or feeling the touch of someone who cares. Any image that promotes warm feelings of love from God is important.
- The need for a sense of identity and meaning in life, of being connected spiritually with God and with all other living beings.
- The need for that which is spiritually familiar: prayers, hymns, poems and other forms that have provided comfort in the past.
- The need for relief from guilt as well as the giving and receiving of forgiveness so as to experience peace with God and others.
- The need to know that one's God is stronger than one's fear of death, an assurance that can be conveyed in part by an experience of care-giving so powerfully positive that the person can die in peace.
- The need to know that God will not punish someone who questions or is angry with him for the suffering, pain and impending death that are experienced. This reaction is often a way for people to come to terms with the realization that life is not fair and that their God and other spiritual people are with them on the journey through dying and that death does not mean failure and is not the enemy.

- The need to have a companion along the journey, a person who is sensitive to the dying person's needs and can be a loving, listening and hugging presence as appropriate to the person.

Most of these are self-evident, but how can we enable those who care to offer help with a sense of identity and meaning in life, especially for those in the last stages of dementia?

Meaning

The idea that 'meaning' has to be found in order for a human to thrive is found in the writings of both Frankl and Erikson. Frankl writes that 'he who has a why to live can bear with almost any how'.[1] While he uses the axis of fulfilment (of meanings) and despair,[2] Erikson uses the axis of integrity (a sense of coherence and wisdom) and despair[3] to describe this search for meaning. They both speak of 'hope' as that which comes from fulfilment[4] and is born of integration,[5] and the absence of these for both writers is 'despair'. For those working with people with dementia, the care offered must aim not just to contain such people so that no harm comes to them, but to enable them to find meaning and integrity in their lives and so to journey into a good death.

How can we enable those with dementia to find meaning?

Our present understanding of dementia is that it cannot be reversed and that, unless treated with drug therapy, the person will, over time, show deterioration in mental, and often physical, faculties. Dementia 'involves brain cell death so that if no other illness were to intervene, it would cause death',[6] but not until 'the individual has lost his memory, his use of language, his ability to dress or feed himself and his personality'.[7] It strips away those human attributes that are valued most: the ability to think, to plan, to remember and to be an active part of society. A carer has written: 'Memory holds the whole of our past life and experience. Its loss is greater than the loss of any of our senses.'[8]

However, those who have dementia are still human beings and as such have been described as 'beings in the world', the world that for everyone must include 'reasons and meanings'.[9] To many, the thought of being without a memory and failing senses can appear horrific. Frankl quotes Albert Camus who says, 'There is but one serious problem, and that is . . . judging whether life is or is not worth living.'[10] The presenting face of someone with dementia can be that they are lost, without a past or a future and often not seeming to know what the present is. Those with dementia could be said to exhibit the characteristics of those who are in despair, that is, with no hope;[11] wandering, staring into space, showing no emotion, having no interaction with others, and undergoing a fragmentation of their personality – a lack of ego-integrity. If we allow ourselves to assume an absence of reason or meaning in their lives, however, then that will affect the care that is offered.

Frankl and Erikson's work on meaning is such that it involves the whole of the person in striving towards integrity. Tom Kitwood was an advocate of alternative approaches to understanding dementia, recognizing that 'the relationship between brain, mind and dementia remains obscure'.[12] Post-mortem examination of those thought to have a greater degree of dementia may show less physical damage than in those whose dementia was 'slight'. This suggests that other factors contribute to the perceived dementia, especially when the 'experiential self', 'an integrated centre grounded in feeling and emotion', has not been well developed. It seems to make the person less able to adapt and make new neural pathways to compensate for the dementia.

Banyard contrasts this model of care that seeks to offer help towards integration with the bio-medical model of care which asks us to look at people as if they were machines. This model suggests that if something goes wrong, then we need to fix the machine. 'It looks for explanations in disordered cells rather than in psychological or social processes.'[13] When applied to the treatment of dementia, the approach is to 'manage' the disease by medication, the problem being the dementing person. For people living in the twentieth century this has some appeal, as we know that some biomedical treatments produce dramatic results. Banyard[14] suggests that Western science has made a distinction between mind and body which encourages us to see people as split in two – a ghost and a biological machine. He says that this view can be comforting to people as they 'think that the original person is still there but trapped in a decaying body'.[15] The thought that the person is blissfully unaware of this change in their being is also of comfort to those who look on, but this may be wishful thinking as the idea that they could be aware would be too painful. One lady recently said to me, 'I am not who I was, I am disintegrating.' For a carer this is a difficult situation. To be there to share the pain of another and to help them towards a meaning in the present, perhaps through the past, and find some hope for the future, is an enormous task.

Banyard suggests a 'bio psychosocial model'[16] which does not look for a single cause or effect, but looks at the connection between mental events and biological changes. Dementia is not a simple disease that can be diagnosed and treated. It is a complex process linking body, brain and the idea of self, and one of the challenges is to find some affirmation of their being in the world, some meaning rather than just existing.

If meaning cannot be found, then this could call into question a person's humanity or 'beingness'. Erikson offers a model which describes the sequence of psychological stages throughout life. His stages define the main struggle within each stage and the psychological strengths that emerge from successful completion of the stage.

Infancy	Trust v mistrust: Hope
1–3 years	Autonomy v shame and doubt: Will
3–6 years	Initiative v guilt: Purpose
6–12 years	Industry v inferiority: Competence
12–18 years	Identity v role confusion: Fidelity
Early adulthood	Intimacy v isolation: Love
Middle age	Creativity v stagnation: Care
Old age	Integrity v despair: Wisdom

(Erikson 1982, 56–7)

Wulff[17] in writing about Erikson's eight stages says of '*Old age*: Integrity versus despair' that, 'there is a quality of closure to a life of integrity, a sense of world order and spiritual meaning', an integrity that seems to convey 'wisdom', which Erikson defines as 'an informed and detached concern with life itself in the face of death itself'.[18]

It is this idea of 'integrity' rather than 'despair' that is the aim of each person as they come to the end of life. Erikson writes: 'Despair expresses the feeling that the time is now short, too short to attempt to start another life and try out alternative roads to integrity'.[19] Integrity on the other hand is the acceptance of 'one's one and only life cycle'[20] as what it is because of the times one has lived through, and that as such they are of value.

Much research is now taking place to develop pharmacological and gene therapy treatments to cure dementia or at least postpone deterioration, but Kitwood, Buckland *et al*[21] showed that high levels of well-being could be observed in those with a whole range of cognitive impairment who were not on controlling medication and '. . . this challenges the views that dementing conditions require the use of psychoactive and tranquilizing medication'.

This suggests the use of psychological therapies in order to find meaning and connection with 'self', yet the idea of using 'therapies' at all on those with dementia is fraught with problems. There are those who would suggest that dealing with dementia and living day to day is in itself enough to cope with. Maslow's hierarchy of needs would lead us to believe that it is only when the lower needs are satisfied that the higher needs can be met.[22] As lower needs are satisfied, higher needs emerge.

Frankl on the other hand[23] suggests that when lower needs are not satisfied, a higher need such as the will to meaning may become even more urgent. He offers the example of those in the German death camps during the Second World War who were deprived of many basic needs, but continued to search for ultimate meaning in their lives. Frankl writes that 'Man's search for meaning is the primary motivation in his life and not a "secondary rationalization" of instinctual drives.'[24]

Eric Erikson speaks of the need for a 'sense of coherence and wholeness'.[25] He says that wisdom 'maintains and learns to convey the integrity of experience in spite of the decline of bodily and mental functions'.[26] This search for meaning and wisdom, despite declining health, within the reality of the present situation of having dementia, necessitates a non-medical care regime.

The three non-medical therapies that are in current usage in the care of those with dementia are Reminiscence Therapy (RT); Reality Orientation (RO); and Validation Therapy (VT). I will give an overview of each therapy, supported by writers in each field, before looking at them in the light of 'meaning', as seen in the work of Frankl and Erikson.

Reminiscence Therapy (RT)

This therapy is usually used in a structured setting, either in groups or one to one, to encourage people to remember what happened in the past. However, it is the 'therapy' most commonly used by those visiting, as people feel on safe ground when talking about the past. The goal of this 're-membering' is to enable older people to identify significant people and events from their past that shaped their life and gave it meaning.[27] It was originally developed for elderly people without dementia, and those who support its use claim that it provides 'an opportunity to review and reorganize events in [their] life'.[28]

RT is popular with professionals such as psychologists and occupational therapists because it does not treat the resident as a 'case', but as an individual who has a history and who, with what remains of their brain function, can be helped to bring that history to mind. Memories help us to perceive ourselves as unique individuals with our own particular experiences, and 'the recalling of past memories enables the person with dementia to remember, even for a short time, the person that they once were'.[29]

It has also been found that RT increased the degree of interaction between staff and patients outside any formal sessions, 'enhancing the morale, attitudes and personal knowledge of their patients by care staff, with consequent improvements in the overall care that patients receive'.[30] This therapy has been found to have the added advantage that it seems to be enjoyed by both residents and carers, especially as it has the 'self' as its focus. It is a working through of a life that has been lived and so holds the key to the person.

Those who live with dementia need help with all aspects of life, and the working through of memories is not different from any other part of their lives. Those who offer this help are in some way helping the person to accept what their life has been, in all its variety, and to come to an acceptance that what has been has been; a working towards an integration of life rather than despair over what might have been.

In this respect those with dementia have much to teach those of us who are 'whole'. Frankl's system of 'logotherapy' – therapy through meaning – holds that 'having been is still a mode of being, perhaps even the safest mode',[31] as the past cannot be taken from a person. Erikson[32] said that at the end, the life-cycle turns back on its beginnings. Hope can be born out of this integration, both for the person and those around them.

Just last week when visiting a family to arrange a funeral I met two brothers. They told me that they did not have a very easy or happy childhood because of their mother, and had, in latter years, become estranged from her. They spoke to me of their experience of their mother with dementia. She was, because of her upbringing, psychologically a needy child so could not offer the boys the mothering they might have expected. But as the dementia developed, so their roles changed and the boys were able to offer her the mothering she had missed out on. As they spoke together of the past and allowed her to explore her memories, they gained an insight into the mother they had not known and this enabled them to be reconciled to her. The dementia had been an opportunity for the mother to reconnect with her past and integrate all that had happened, and for the boys to share love for the first time.

The working through of memories had helped all three of them towards the closure of one life, and when she died they were able to mourn the mother they had lost. They told me that their lives were richer as a result of the opportunities that dementia had given them to work through together the problems in the past and gain meaning from them.

Frankl writes that there is a 'healing force' in meaning, and the brothers' experience of finding meaning with their mother while she had dementia are echoed in his words: 'How happy we were that we could experience this close contact for those last few weeks, and how poor we would have been if . . . [she] had died from a heart attack lasting a few seconds.'[33]

Reality Orientation (RO)

Reality Orientation originated in 1958 when Dr James Folson instituted a programme of activity for elderly patients in the Veterans Administration Hospital in Topeka, Kansas, USA. It was developed as a means of 'orientating a person to their environment by means of constant stimulation' (Miller 1993, 120). It is commonly understood as a means of stimulating unused neurological pathways in order to compensate for brain damage. Those who use RO support its use on the grounds that 'it improves the quality of life for dementia sufferers'[34] and enables carers and staff to provide a 'treatment package'.

The aim is to correct confused speech, reinforcing correct and appropriate usage of words, and constantly to remind the resident what their name is, where they are, what the current time is and what events are in the news. Inappropriate behaviour is also corrected, with correct behaviour prompted and encouraged.

Apart from direct interaction with the staff, RO can be seen in signs, using both words and symbols, which give a 'cue' to the resident to enable them to bring the meaning to mind. This is especially useful on the doors of toilets and in the use of information boards which can have the day, date, what the weather is like and what activities are planned for that day in the home. It is not so useful when everyday objects in the home are labelled or when words and actions are linked. The problem with this is that it can cause 'information overload' and so, instead of bringing meaning to a world that has become confused, it can reinforce disconnection.

There are those who ask why we should bother to force reality on people with dementia, as many of them seem content to sit and watch the world go by, if they are aware of the world at all. In fact forcing reality on to such people could be said to be a form of cruelty. However, if all people are recognized as being of value, then there is a necessity to affirm their humanity in the time that they live.

The past is important, as it is through our unique history that we become the people we are. But if the past only means something when still remembered, 'it becomes a subjective misinterpretation of our ontology of time'.[35] There is a sense in which those who are encouraged to live in the past are hardly living, as they are not aware of the present. There is a need for all people to find meaning in life as they are experiencing it. To those who would ask 'Why bother?', Frankl says, 'Faced with life's transitoriness we may say that the future does not yet exist; the past does not exist any more; and the only thing that really exists is the present.'[36] Erikson writes of the use of the pronoun 'I' as being a 'verbal assurance that each of us [is] in a centre of awareness in the centre of the universe . . . in other words we are alive and aware of it'.[37]

Reality Orientation needs to be used sensitively but has its place and is confirmed by the writings of Frankl and Erikson. One cannot change the place and time that is lived in, but one can be aware of and find some meaning and integrity in the present moment. The 'sacrament of the present moment' is this idea in Christian thought. After all, we only have one life, and this moment is all that truly exists.

Frankl writes of the transitory nature of all that is and the 'present being the borderline between the unreality of the future and the eternal reality of the past'.[38] The past he sees as eternal because 'no one can blot out what has been'.[39] So, no part of life is seen as worthless or lacking in meaning.

Validation Therapy (VT)

This was developed by Naomi Feil in 1966 as a reaction to insensitive use of Reality Orientation. She had been working with disoriented elderly people, her job being to help them to face reality and relate to others in the group. She found that helping them to face reality was unrealistic, and said that they 'withdrew or became increasingly hostile whenever I tried to orient them to an intolerable present reality'.[40]

The ethos of Validation Therapy is that people must be listened to where they are and that there is little advantage in correcting people's language when it has suffered as a result of dementia, while letting their feelings go unheard. Validation is used to empathize with another, to walk with them in their journey into dementia. Feil teaches that validating another's feelings builds trust which in turn brings safety and renews a sense of worth. To validate someone with dementia means to pick up their clues and help put their feelings into words.

The advantages of this therapy are that it acknowledges that the resident is a unique individual and that there is reason behind the often confused language and what could be seen as irrational or frightening behaviour. Wilder Penfield said:

When recent memory (short-term memory) fails, very old humans restore the balance by retrieving early memories. When eyesight fails, they use the mind's eye to see. When hearing goes, they listen to sounds from the past.[41]

Those with dementia relive their past to restore their dignity, to remember a time when they were someone whom they recognize.

Feil[42] uses Erik Erikson's Theory of Life Stages and Tasks to explain how Validation can help with resolving the final stage of life. Erikson's theory is that there are tasks to be accomplished at each stage of life and that success in accomplishing a task at a certain age will depend on how well previous stages have been accomplished. 'Fears that were never faced in childhood reappear in disguise in old age.'

The task in old age according to Erikson's theory is to review life, to tie up living and to find inner strength which will lead to integrity. Failure to accomplish the task will lead to despair, the feeling that I might as well be dead. Integrity in old age is the ability to use deep self-respect to heal the bruises that come with age. Without this self-acceptance, if no one can be trusted to love you, there is only despair. If despair is ignored, then it can turn into depression; anger which is locked away.

But Feil suggests that there is a stage beyond 'Integrity versus despair', one of 'Resolution versus vegetation'.[43] This stage belongs to the old–old. The task that is theirs to accomplish is to sort out the unresolved feelings of their past ready for their final move. She says that to die in peace is a deep human need. When people are told that they have only so much time to live, it is often seen as the time to put things right so that, with issues resolved, they might die in peace.

Frankl writes of the importance of seeing the person as a human being of worth and value. Those with dementia are no different in that respect from all other human beings and need someone to listen to and to validate their feelings. If no one listens then they withdraw and vegetate, becoming one of the living dead who can be seen in many residential homes. It is through this human contact of someone listening to the meaning behind their words and actions that those with dementia are able to cope and find meaning.

However, Stokes and Goudie maintain[44] that this form of therapy remains a relatively untried and unproven method of counselling in terms of both its underlying premises and principles of practice. They have taken the ideas behind Erikson's eighth stage of 'Integrity versus despair' further and what they suggest is 'resolution therapy', which they introduced in 1989. The underlying premise of this therapy is that in people suffering from an organic dementia, the disoriented messages received and the confused behaviour observed are likely to be attempts to make sense of what is happening now, or efforts to make their needs known which, if ignored, can result in people being labelled as difficult. They suggest the use of counselling skills so that carers can 'empathize with hidden meanings and feelings'[45] which lie behind confused speech and actions. This is a therapeutic approach which reaches behind a person's memory to acknowledge their emotions as they struggle to cope with their situation. This idea is very similar to Feil's life stage of 'Resolution versus vegetation' from which she developed her Validation Therapy. Both these therapies look to find meaning behind the words used, and both develop Erikson's work to offer therapy for those with cognitive difficulties.

Summing up

Having considered the range of therapies used in relation to the ideas offered by Frankl and Erikson, I find that these writers' thoughts on 'meaning' support and validate the approach used to care for those with dementia. I also find that their ideas are being developed in such a way that they are even more suited to good dementia care.

Each person's situation is different, and from the outside we can only guess the difficulty of coping with dementia, but it need not be hopeless. Writing of his experience in a concentration camp during the Second World War, when everything was taken from them until they thought they could no longer exist, Frankl says 'a man can get used to anything, but do not ask us how'.[46] Frankl coped by trying to make sense of his situation and finding a meaning that would hold him.

Frankl sees the human search for meaning as the primary drive in life. Erikson's eight stages of life give us one way in which meaning is worked out in the different stages of life. For both writers this 'meaning' can give an integrity to the person such that value is added to life. This work of finding meaning can be fulfilled by the person herself, but for those with dementia the work has to be done with the help of others. Frankl's major contribution to the debate is 'logotherapy' – therapy through meaning – which is offered to those with dementia whenever the different therapies noted above are used as they all find their basis in the idea of the value of the individual.

These two writers offer much to the care of those with dementia: Erikson through his work on the life-cycle and the tasks of each stage of life and especially the last stage of 'Integrity versus despair', and Frankl who learned by personal experience the vital importance of finding meaning in life, for without that there is nothing.

We cannot answer the question 'Why?', especially when that refers to dementia. But we can, with careful attention, offer such care that meaning and integrity can be found and so enable the journey into a good death.

Notes

1 Frankl, V., *Man's Search for Meaning*, Beacon Press, 1992, p. 9.
2 Frankl, V., *The Unheard Cry for Meaning*, Hodder & Stoughton, 1979, p. 42.
3 Erikson, E., *The Life Cycle Completed: A Review*, W W Norton, 1982.
4 Frankl, V., 1992, op. cit., p. 11.
5 Erikson, E., 1982, op. cit., p. 26.
6 Gidley, I. and Shears, R., *Alzheimer's: What it is and How to Cope*, Unwin Hyman Ltd, 1988, p. 18.
7 Dippel, R. L., 'The Caregivers' in Dippel, R. L. and Hutton, J. T. (eds), *Caring for the Alzheimer's Patient*, Prometheus Books, 1996, pp. 11–27 at 12.
8 Gibbons, T. (1995) *Observations and Reflections of a Carer*, Scarsdale Books, 1995, p. 3.
9 Frankl, V., 1979, op. cit., p. 52.
10 Ibid, p. 23.
11 Ryecroft, C., *Despair: A Critical Dictionary of Psychoanalysis*, Penguin, 1995, p. 37.
12 Harding, N. and Palfrey, C., *The Social Construction of Dementia: Confused Professionals*, Jessica Kingsley, 1997, p. 59.
13 Banyard, P., *Applying Psychology to Health*, Hodder & Stoughton, 1999, p. 4.
14 Ibid, p. 4.
15 Ibid, p. 5
16 Ibid, p. 6.
17 Wulff, D. M., *Psychology of Religion: Classic and Contemporary Views*, John Wiley & Sons, 1991, p. 378.
18 Erikson, E., 1982, op. cit., p. 61.
19 Erikson, E., *Childhood and Society*, Triad/Granada, 1981, p. 242.
20 Ibid., p. 241.
21 Kitwood, T., Buckland, S. and Petre, T., *Brighter Futures: A Report on Research into Provision for Persons with Dementia in Residential Homes, Nursing Homes and Sheltered Housing*, Anchor Housing, 1995, p. 34.
22 Maslow, A., *Motivation and Personality*, Harper & Row, 1970.
23 Frankl, V., 1979, op. cit., p. 33.
24 Frankl, V., 1992, op. cit., p. 105.
25 Erikson, E., 1982, op. cit., p. 65.
26 Erikson, E., *Vital Involvement in Old Age*, Norton & Co Ltd, 1986, p. 37.
27 Ronch, J. L. G. and Joseph, A., *Mental Wellness in Ageing*, Health Professions Press, 2003, p. 240.
28 Miller, E., *The Psychology of Dementia*, John Wiley & Sons, 1993, p. 127.
29 Goldsmith, M., 1996, *Hearing the Voice of People with Dementia*, Jessica Kingsley, 1996, p. 95.
30 Pulsford, D., 'Therapeutic Activities for People with Dementia: What, Why . . . and Why Not?', *Journal of Advanced Nursing*, 26, 1997, pp. 704–9 at 707.
31 Frankl, V., 1979, op. cit., p. 105.
32 Erikson, E., 1982, op. cit., p. 62.
33 Frankl, V., 1979, op. cit., pp. 21–2.
34 Miller, E., 1993, op. cit., p. 120.
35 Frankl, V., *Psychotherapy and Existentialism: Selected Papers on Logo-Therapy*, Vintage Books, 1978, p. 106.
36 Ibid, p. 102.

37 Erikson, E., 1986, op. cit., p. 52.
38 Frankl, V., 1978, op. cit., p. 111.
39 Ibid, p. 107.
40 Feil, N., *Validation: The Feil Method*, Edward Feil Publications, 1992, p. 9.
41 Ibid, p. 12.
42 Ibid, p. 12.
43 Ibid, p. 18.
44 Stokes, G. and Goudie, F., 'Counselling Confused Elderly People' in Stokes, G. and Goudie, F. (eds), *Working with Dementia*, Winslow Press, 1990, pp. 181–90 at 183.
45 Ibid, p. 185.
46 Frankl, V., 1992, op. cit., p. 30.

Chapter 12

Achieving a Good Death in Dementia

BEATRICE GODWIN

Beatrice Godwin is a social worker and trainer currently working as an assertive inreach worker in a community mental health team for older adults. This new project aims to resolve mental health crises among older adults in residential and nursing care. She has also been funded by Avon and Wiltshire Mental Health Partnership NHS Trust to research 'Hospice-type Care for People with Dementia', looking at well-being for people with dementia at the end of their lives. She brings her skill as a reflective practitioner to bear upon this final piece on what a good death might mean. As we read it, we might reflect upon what a good death might mean for us.

I'm going to tell you the story of Dora and her dying days, in the way it was told to me by her caring, professional daughter.

> Mother had dementia. She was doubly incontinent, babbled all the time, she didn't know who any of us were, and she couldn't understand what we said. She was not conscious in any meaningful way at all. She had pneumonia, but, as she had been a marathon runner, her heart was very strong. She was admitted to hospital but took thirteen days to die. My sister said: 'The trouble with our mother is that she doesn't know she is dying. Otherwise, she would have turned her face to the wall and just died, but she keeps going, like an automaton. Her heart just keeps on beating.'

My informant went on:

> The whole atmosphere of a hospital is just about looking after the living. It's difficult for the relatives, too. You carry on as though the dying person is there, even though he or she is not responding. The

family has to cope with all the petty emotional and practical problems that emerge at this time on top of everything else. So you go through the motions of caring, even though the whole thing is a charade from the point of view of the person who is dying. What you do is only done for the benefit of the relatives.

Dora's family is typical of many loving and caring families all over the Western world. They obviously tried their utmost to do their best for Dora. Any death is emotionally draining for all concerned. I believe that to have a relative dying of dementia is especially difficult.

In my opinion, there are five obstacles to a good death in dementia.

1 The practicalities

A death of or with dementia usually takes place in residential, nursing care or hospital. This has added problems: who does the hands-on care, can the family stay out of normal visiting hours and will they be in the way?

The death of an elderly relative can be especially taxing – often miles from home and superimposed on a busy work schedule, with no such provision as 'terminal leave'. (Why not, I wonder? Should we be lobbying for this?)

For the death of someone with dementia, there are huge additional problems. If even an intelligent, well-educated, loving and caring family like Dora's can't see a role for themselves in helping her with her dying, then we are faced with an uphill struggle. Burgener[1] comments, 'Caregivers [of people with dementia] are often at a loss to define positive ways to help maintain quality of life.' This problem is clearly exacerbated when the person is dying. Dora's family are a microcosm of society, where dementia care is summed up in the slogan: 'Alzheimer's disease. No cure. No care. No hope!'

If there is anything worse than living with dementia, it is dying with dementia. It involves the twin taboos of death and dementia, neither of which are topics we can easily talk through with friends.

2 The attitudes of professionals

How is dementia perceived by doctors and other health-care professionals? I described how difficult it could be for families to find a role in caring for someone with dementia. Many in the medical profession are equally surrounded by this 'cloud of unknowing'. Only last year, I heard a consultant psychiatrist say at a conference: 'The person who is loved is gone before their eventual death.' Others speak of dementia as 'a death that leaves the body behind'.

The prognosis in dementia is described as a one-way street – exclusively one way, and that is down. This view is shared by many nurses and carers. This school of thought believes that there is no point in trying to offer solace to a person with dementia, because the person is 'a cipher, a shadow, a shell'. It is paralleled by the conventional wisdom expressed in the euthanasia debate. Dora's state is seen as worse than dead. We would not keep animals alive in that state. Putting her out of her misery would be more appropriate.

3 How attitudes impact on the care given to people with dementia

The third difficulty for Dora's family is that these attitudes have consequences in terms of the interpersonal care that is offered. The type of care that is offered can in turn lead to negative consequences. Dora's state could be what is described as 'vegetative'. Arguably, a vegetative state may be psychological rather than physical. The care offered to someone who appears to be in a vegetative state would only make matters worse: 'Vegetation, which according to conventional wisdom is the end point, may be understood psychologically as a state of very severe ill-being: the individual has lost almost all that remained of self-esteem, agency, social confidence and hope, and withdrawn into terminal apathy and despair.'[2]

4 The social policy which underpins the delivery of care

The fourth difficulty for Dora and her relatives is that attitudes stem from social policy. By default, our social policy prescribes a lack of responsiveness to the needs of people with dementia. Our social work practice echoes this approach. The lives of people with dementia are seen as having no value. They should merely be stored in 'care' warehouses, waiting rooms for death – in T. S. Eliot's words, 'Living and partly living'. They are moved from their own home to a care home, from a residential home to an EMI (specialist dementia) home, maybe on to a nursing home, or even an EMI nursing home, then often to hospital, to die. Each move, for people with dementia, only serves to confound their disorientation, confusion and isolation.

Community care is a sham when it claims to be 'needs-led': in reality it is budget-driven. If you are poor but want to die at home, tough luck! Your needs will be costed and the budget compared against the net cost policy. If residential care can be bought cheaper than your help at home, you are highly likely to be moved on to a care home, whether you wish it or not. You and your 'package of care' (the bundle of what remains of your life) will be bought and sold. You will be passed down the ladder of humanity, one rung at a time.

This is more complex and even more devastating for people with dementia. Because of their alleged lack of 'mental capacity', they are seen as unable to exercise the illusory 'choice' of which community care boasts. They can't argue their case. And they are the ones least able to cope with change.

Liz Lloyd,[3] a researcher on dying in old age, identifies these key themes: promoting non-institutional services, encouraging openness about illness and dying, enabling older people to exercise choice and control over caring interventions, minimizing older people's fear of death and maintaining family and other social networks. Our national policy on dementia care has a very long way to go before it can aspire to meet any of these goals.

In the same paper, Lloyd points out that the Report of the UK Royal Commission on Long Term Care[4] emphasizes the goal of 'independence as an overriding policy aim'. She maintains that this aim 'implies an abhorrence of conditions of dependency and of the need for care'. This is highly significant in relation to caring for people who are dying and those whose physical and mental state places them in a position of dependence on others.

5 Medical practice

The fifth obstacle to Dora and her family achieving a good death is medical practice. Our social policy may be seen as misguided, and medical practice can be just as unenlightened. In one study, McCarthy et al.,[5] found that patients with dementia had very similar care needs to patients with cancer. There was one major difference between the two groups of patients: people with dementia had more symptoms than cancer patients. These symptoms were pain, low mood, constipation, loss of appetite, confusion and urinary incontinence. The research also mentions that the room where they spent most of their time or died was 'not at all peaceful and quiet'. Patients with dementia can't speak out. They can't ask for palliative care, and they don't get it.

Lloyd-Williams[6] also shows that the palliative care needs of 'end-stage patients with advanced dementia are not being met in hospitals and nursing homes'. Julia Addington-Hall[7] has raised awareness of the need for palliative care for people with dementia. There are very practical problems, such as the fact that people can die with dementia and/or of dementia. Hospices manage their workload by being able to predict their patients' life expectancy. Unlike typical hospice patients, the time patients with dementia will take to die is unusually difficult to predict. Their 'dying trajectory' does not follow a pattern, although there is research which attempts to outline one with some measure of success.[8] Obviously, we cannot magic dementia hospices into existence, but what can be done is to introduce palliative care into settings where people with dementia die.

Another piece of research[9] documents current practice where medical treatment for people with dementia was radically worse than for the control group who were cognitively intact. When patients with dementia were subjected to moderately to severely painful and uncomfortable procedures such as insertion of a catheter, mechanical ventilation and physical restraint, they were only offered half the amount of analgesia which was offered to the non-demented patients. Only one-quarter had a standing order for analgesics. Patients with dementia were not given appropriate levels of painkillers, and there was no evidence of palliative care.

Dora's state was described by her family as 'not conscious in any meaningful way at all'. This state could have been drug induced. Age Concern and the Royal College of Physicians have both published research on the overuse of anti-psychotic drugs, which have been dubbed 'chemical coshes' because of their heavy sedative effects. There is evidence that their use on people with dementia can hasten their cognitive decline and even their death.[10] There is ample evidence of this prejudiced attitude on the part of some in the medical profession, some of whom may need to be shown Burgener's[11] evidence that 'decreased discomfort states in the Alzheimer's disease patient . . . have been shown to increase the patient's positive affect, thus improving psychological well-being'. In plain English, this can be summed up as: being comfortable cheers people up, even if they have dementia!

If we could suspend our disbelief for a moment, we could imagine that Dora, near the end of her life, might comment on the medical treatment she received by paraphrasing Shakespeare's Merchant of Venice. She might say:

> Hath not a person with dementia eyes? If you prick us, do we not bleed? Hath we not hands, organs, dimensions, senses, affections, passions, fed with the same food, hurt by the same medical procedures, subject to the same diseases, healed by the same means, warmed and cooled by the same summer and winter as another man is?

What goes wrong, that we can no longer recognize our fellow humanity in a person with dementia? It is the same problem that used to blight the care of people with learning disabilities. It is a sort of cortical arrogance, or what Kitwood has called hypercognitivism.[12] It is a valuing of people according to the functions of their brain, ignoring the rest of their personality. It is nothing more than the everyday phrase: 'Where there's no sense, there's no feeling.'

Michael Ignatieff[13] conveys something of that unrecognized place when writing about his mother: 'Occasionally, her pacing ceases, her hunted look is conjured away . . . by watching sunlight stream through the trees, and I see something pass over her face that looks like serenity . . .'

Surmounting the obstacles

So now, today, have we come to a place where we might be able to look for a better future for people with dementia, where we might be able to help them find some sort of serenity? How can we begin to surmount these obstacles? Cicely Saunders comments that we should 'help people live until they die', also sometimes quoted as 'live well until they die'. Can that include people with dementia, too? What should be our guidelines for achieving this? Counsel and Care's booklet, *Last Rites*,[14] pinpoints three cornerstones of good practice. These are very simple: honesty, non-isolation and communication. Honesty is a huge challenge, given the communication difficulties inherent in dementia. Non-isolation and communication are definitely suitable aspirations in end-of-life care in dementia. Social policy which incorporated these two goals would be a lot more humane.

We can challenge the dehumanizing approach to dementia by following Kitwood's guidance.[15] Kitwood, a psychologist and a philosopher, shows us how 'personhood' can be maintained by offering person-centred dementia care. He describes this as 'much more than meeting basic physical needs' [if only . . . as we have seen, people with dementia are quite far from being offered parity of basic treatment] '. . . attending to the whole person, enabling each individual to make the fullest use of his or her abilities and to remain a social being'.

He teaches us how to challenge what Lawton[16] calls 'the stripping of personhood that is common in Alzheimer's patients and the resulting demoralizing effect this has on both institutional and family carers'. (For anyone who needs a book with practical advice, I recommend Jim Marr's[17] chapter on dying.)

Kitwood describes the effects of dementia and sums them up as an equation:

$$D = P \text{ and } LH \text{ and } H \text{ and } SP \text{ and } NI$$

The effects of dementia (D) are a combination of the person's personality (P), life history (LH), health (H), and here I would include sensory impairment, that is blindness and deafness, because they are so prevalent in this age group and so crucial in the way in which they compound the effects of dementia. Then there is the social psychology (SP) of the care offered. All of the above are as important or more important than the actual neurological impairment (NI), that is the damage to the brain. This relative downgrading of the importance of the damage to the brain is borne out by post-mortem changes in the brain, the extent of which does not correlate with the person's ability to function prior to death. In other words, there is no relation between the damage to a person's brain cells and their quality of life.

How would Kitwood's equation help Dora and her family? Dora's family should have been helped to work through Dora's needs in a positive and proactive way, using Kitwood's formula.

Personality

What was her personality? Was she an anxious and agitated person; if so, how could she be soothed? Was she a fighter, in which case her family could talk about all she had achieved in her life, to try to help her rest on her laurels and let go. Hearing is said to be the last sense to go.[18] We all know that a warm, friendly human voice can be reassuring and comforting, even if we are drifting off to sleep and not taking in what is said. Drifting off into sleep, into dementia and into death may feel the same.

Life history

What was Dora's life history? If she was a marathon runner, did she love fresh air? Could we ensure that she has a welcome and refreshing breeze from outside blowing away the suffocating central heating? What do her family remember of her tastes and preferences? Does she have a favourite fragrant flower? We could waft it under her nose. Who knows? She might still enjoy it. Speaking of the senses, there are tastes and textures, sounds and sights which may still please. For religious believers, ritual often offers a panoply of sensual experience: incense, music, laying on of hands, candles, Communion bread and wine. All of these also have the comforting benefit of tapping in to long-term memory and rote learning, which can remain intact even in the most profound dementia.

Most of all, people with dementia, in their journey into darkness, almost all love to hold your hand[19] and see your smile, or if you want it in research-speak: 'Significant correlations were found between the caregiver's smiling behaviours and the patient's calm/functional behaviours.'[20]

Health

How is Dora's general health? If she has pneumonia, we can all empathize with her pain and discomfort. What practical measures will help with this? She will need to have all the assistance that palliative care can offer.

Burgener[21] writes: 'Other experiences still available to the late stage Alzheimer's patient that may impact on psychological well-being include pain or comfort experiences, need for positive stimulation (interpersonal and environmental), individualized touch experiences, amelioration of depressive states and spiritual support.' Other researchers[22] found that 87 per cent of patients with Alzheimer's disease suffered from depression. Depression can mimic dementia, just as a high temperature or thyroid imbalance can cause confusion. Depression can be treated, even in dementia.

Social psychology

What is the social psychology of the hospital ward where she is receiving care? Communication is a huge issue! Beware of the 'gobbledegook' phenomenon! Do not assume that the person's speech never makes sense. Be alert to the possibility that the person may have lucid intervals and that communication may be metaphorical.

Killick, a poet who works with people with dementia, quotes insightful comments made by people with dementia who are close to death.[23] By listening carefully, we can minimize the disabling effects of Dora's neurological impairment – her actual dementia. Even if she appears not to understand, we can give her the benefit of the doubt. We can explain what is happening in clear, simple, audible language:

'The nurse is going to wash you now.'
'Show me where it hurts.'
'It's night time now, so you can sleep.'

We must avoid at all costs the 'malignant social psychology' and 'personal detractions' which Kitwood describes and which are a daily occurrence in many care homes and hospitals; for example, two staff talking to each other over your bed can be disconcerting and even disorientating. Sitting up in bed can be a slow process and immensely confusing when you have forgotten how to sit up. You need lots of time and individualized support and prompts to master this forgotten skill, not an abrupt imperative, 'Sit up!' or someone yanking your arm.

Recently, common personal detraction has been highlighted: the staff who put your drink and your dinner down and leave you to fend for yourself, even when you have forgotten what a fork is or even what food is for.

For everyone with dementia, we need a specialism of dementia care which can look at that whole range of 'living until you die'.

Kitwood[24] shows that, with good person-centred care, the scientifically impossible notion of 'rementing' can occur. People can and do appear less confused and demented when they are in receipt of good quality care. One aim of research into a good death for people with dementia must be to try to improve the quality of their life, right up to the end.

Kitwood, as always, puts it beautifully:

> It is essential for us [that is, people with dementia] to know that there are others with a clear sense of who we are, what we are feeling, what gives us joy, what causes us pain and fear. When we are going through times of great trouble, when we are burdened with stress or low in spirits, we especially need to be understood. Without that precious gift, which only others can bestow, we are moving to the edge of madness. For to be mad ... is to be no longer in real communication with other living beings, to be utterly alone.

Research is needed to find out how we can begin to take away this sensation of the edge of madness, the utter aloneness of dying with dementia.

Notes

1 Burgener, S.,'Quality of Life in Late Stage Dementia' in Volicer, L. and Hurley, A. (eds), *Hospice Care for Advanced, Progressive Dementia*, Springer, 1998, p. 110.

2 Kitwood, T., 'Towards a Theory of Dementia Care: The Interpersonal Process', *Ageing and Society,* 13, 1993, pp. 51–67.

3 Lloyd, L., 'Dying in Old Age: Promoting Well-being at the End of life', *Mortality,* 5 (2), 2000, pp. 171–88.

4 Royal Commission on Long Term Care, *With Respect to Old Age: Long Term Care – Rights and Responsibilities,* The Stationery Office, 1999, p. 81.

5 McCarthy et al, 'Experience of Dying with Dementia, a Retrospective Study', *International Journal of Geriatric Psychiatry,* 12, 1997, pp. 404–9.

6 Lloyd-Williams, M., 'An Audit of Palliative Care in Dementia', *European Journal of Cancer Care,* 5, 1996, pp. 53–5.

7 Addington-Hall, J., 'Positive Partnerships: Palliative Care for Adults with Severe Mental Health Problems' Occasional Paper 17, 2000, National Council for Hospice and Specialist Palliative Care Services.

8 Morrison, R. and Siu, A., 'Survival in End-stage Dementia following Acute Illness', *JAMA,* 284 (1), 2000, pp. 47–52.

9 Ahronheim, J. et al, 'Treatment of the Dying in the Acute Care Hospital', *Archives of Internal Medicine,* 156 (18), 1996, pp. 2094–100.

10 Winchester, R., 'The Wrong Prescription', *Community Care Magazine,* 9–15 August 2001.

11 Burgener, 1998, op. cit.

12 Kitwood, T. and Bredin, K., 'Towards a Theory of Dementia Care: Personhood and Well-being', *Ageing and Society*, 12, 1992, p. 278.

13 Ignatieff, M., *Scar Tissue*, Vintage, 1992.

14 Counsel and Care, *Last Rites*, 1995.

15 Loveday, B. and Kitwood, T., *Improving Dementia Care*, University of Bradford Dementia Group and Hawker Publications, 1998.

16 Lawton, M., 'Quality of Life in Alzheimer's Disease', *Alzheimer's Disease and Associated Disorders*, 8, Supplement 3, 1995, pp. 138–50.

17 Marr, J., 'Loss, Bereavement and Care of the Dying' in Benson, Sue (ed.), 'The Care Assistant's Guide to Working with People with Dementia', *Journal of Dementia Care*, 1998.

18 Ibid.

19 Ibid.

20 Burgener, 1998, op. cit.

21 Ibid.

22 Merriam et al, 'The Psychiatric Symptoms of Alzheimer's Disease', *Journal of American Geriatrics Society*, 36, 1988, pp. 7–12.

23 Killick, J. and Allan, K., *Communication and the Care of People with Dementia, Great Britain*, Open University Press, 2001.

24 Kitwood, T., *Dementia Reconsidered*, Oxford University Press, 1997.

Afterword

In September 1990, Archbishop George Carey gave an interview to the *Reader's Digest*, in which he was asked to describe how he saw the Church today. He said he hoped that the Church would grow progressively younger. The Church today seemed to him rather like a very old grandmother who sat by the chimney-breast muttering to herself, ignored by the rest of the family and out of touch with her culture.

This image, used by a chief pastor, could be said to be typical of the Churches' ageism, with which we pastors collude. We seem unable to embrace and affirm an all-age Church, within which older people are valued partners. These essays have asked the reader to think again about dementia within the context of old age. Our ageism and fear combine to make dementia a particularly complex pastoral challenge.

We deal with our fears about illness in a variety of ways. Consider how we responded to HIV in the late twentieth century. We find it hard to engage with those who are different. We fear contagion. It has also taken a long time for us to face the cruel reality of cancer, and to discover a humane way of engaging with the whole person and their pain. We do not like to think of ourselves as vulnerable. Now another challenge faces us. They call it the long goodbye. If each of us were ever in the situation of being able to choose the shape of our diminishments, a physical one might be easier to bear than a mental one. Dementia strikes fear in people's hearts, and with good reason.

Diagnosing dementia is often difficult, but the steady progression of memory loss can be devastating for all those involved in care. There are currently 700,000 people in the UK living with dementia, and the number is likely to rise to more than one million by 2025. About 60,000 deaths a year are attributable to dementia. The financial cost to the UK is more than £17 billion a year. There is no cure. Current treatments alleviate symptoms temporarily, at best. Caring for someone with dementia is stressful, physically and emotionally draining, and very expensive.

The implications of all this present a challenge to us and to the shape of our communities. After the best-selling novelist Terry Pratchett was diagnosed with early-onset Alzheimer's, he said:

> It's a strange life when you 'come out' – people get embarrassed, lower their voices, and get lost for words . . . What is needed is will and determination. The first step is to talk about dementia because it's a fact, well enshrined in folklore, that if we are to kill the demon, then first we have to say its name. (Interview with *BBC News*, 10 June 2008)

This reinforces surveys that suggest that those living with dementia suffer stigma. A report from the Alzheimer's Society says that some people see neighbours crossing the street to avoid them. The fear that surrounds dementia is bound up with our inability to engage with ageing in ourselves and others. The Church reflects this ageism, and little priority is given to older people and their needs. What is needed is investment in awareness campaigns. Government, charities, churches and employers need to work together to offer support and information.

There are many innovations in this area of care that challenge us to develop better practice. The distinguished psychologist Oliver James, in his book *Contented Dementia*,[1] takes the reader into the world of the self, and the way the disease strips away memory, dignity and hope. He shows that dementia need not be a nightmare of frustration and embarrassment. In an approach that puts the person at the heart of care, through sensitive and radical listening, Professor James shows that it is possible to unlock isolation and distress.

It is often best to retain some of the security of a familiar environment, he suggests. A Memory Box containing meaningful items that say something about the individual can help those with memory loss. It can be a starting point for conversation, and a challenge to carers to see an older person's individuality. A packet of seeds is a prompt for memories about gardens, for example. Let us look at the person who shaped this book.

By all accounts, Dorothy Johnson was quite a woman. An international bridge player and an imaginative social organizer, she was entrepreneurial in the way she thought and was fun to be with. She also succeeded in being best friend to her daughter, Penny. And, as Penny Garner puts it, if your best friend says something, you pay attention.

So when, at 59, Dorothy started to show symptoms of dementia and simultaneously to provide illuminating shafts of information about what was happening to her, Penny watched and listened hard. Like her mother, she was intrigued. She remembers the day Dorothy, feeling agitated, stood in her kitchen holding a list of reminders written for her by her concerned – and highly organized – husband.

'She looked at us and said, "Can you explain what is the point of writing these lists if I'm not going to remember to read them?"' On another occasion at Penny's home, Dorothy brandished a milk bottle and asked where the fridge was. 'I wouldn't be asking if I didn't need the information', she explained.

Over five years or so, Penny made a series of observations that has enabled her to develop a radical new treatment for all forms of dementia. Called SPECAL, Specialized Early Care for Alzheimer's, which is also the name of her charity, based in Burford in Oxfordshire, it revolves around her insight that while people who have dementia cannot store new facts, they can store new feelings.

'As we all run on what's just happened, and they can't store new facts, their fuel is feelings', she points out. 'It's abundantly clear that feelings are more important than facts to the person with dementia.'

This means that when a well-meaning carer points out to the person that they have forgotten something – say, to post a letter – they feel embarrassed and agitated. They have been unable to store the new information about needing to post the letter, but because they have been confronted with this fact, of which they have no knowledge, their overwhelming feeling is that they are not in control. Penny's therapy is designed to cut out the confrontation that causes the person with dementia to dwell on negative emotions, so that even though they can't remember what has just happened, they feel content.

In many ways Specal is an unlikely therapy. Its creator may be extremely bright, charismatic and intuitive, but she is also a Cotswolds granny in her mid-sixties who has no medical or nursing qualifications, just the confidence to make up her own rules based on 30 years of working with people who have dementia.

And Specal can seem counterintuitive. Conventional logic may tell us to try to orientate a person who has dementia by reminding them that today is Monday and they have forgotten to do something. Much better not to challenge them, Penny suggests. Instead bypass what they can't remember and tune in to their long-term memory, which is still functioning, as brain scans have proved, and use that to make emotional connections that enable them to make sense of the present.

'They haven't lost their ability to reason, they've lost the information that other people around them are using to reason with', she says. 'But they do have some substitute stuff in their memory. My mother could recall stacks of stuff, and when she did that she was confident. She would make an intelligent match between what she saw and old facts. Sitting in the doctor's waiting room, she would think she was at an airport and ask if our flight had been called. If I said, "Not yet", she was happy.

'But by challenging her, my father could reduce her very easily to a dithering wreck. I began to see that there were facts that she could access in her memory, but that she couldn't reach them when she was stressed. She was showing me that she could be two different people: one the person who had always been there, the other deranged. My mother was in there and she was unchanged if she was in touch with language and information that she understood.'

Penny uses the metaphor of a photograph album. The photographs represent memories that we all have and that we use to make sense of what is happening to us. For someone with dementia the recent pages are blank, the old pages much more complete.

Specal focuses on this stored information, which relates to the past when the person was capable and felt in control, and uses that to engender feelings of well-being. Doing this relies on understanding an individual's past, especially their enthusiasms, and plugging in to what's there, protecting them from needing new information. If someone enjoyed growing vegetables, ferreting out the expressions they use that relate to that and using them regularly not only enables them to make sense of what is happening to them, but makes them feel safe, in control and induces calm. Something like showing them a packet of seeds or saying, 'The carrots will be coming along nicely', can be used to get them to a table for a meal, or to the bathroom.

Above all, Penny insists, don't ask questions, don't contradict. 'That throws them onto today's page of pictures, which is blank, so they don't have the answers. It's as though their memory is an artificial leg. If you argue with them about their inability to recall the present you're kicking that away, pointing out their disability and rendering them incompetent. The carer has to understand that it's he or she who has got to change.'

Isn't it unethical to collude with people who think they are waiting for a flight when they are in the doctor's surgery? 'Which is the more unethical?' Penny counters. 'To insist that they find something that isn't in their memory? Or to use what they have got and make as good a match as they can?'

'In psychiatric terms, there is a world of difference between somebody claiming to be Queen Victoria, and somebody describing a memory', she says. 'If somebody is experiencing a past in their present and that is giving them well-being, where is the ethical case for potentially starting off a cycle of loss of self-confidence and fear of madness? That's what happens when you impose your version of reality on theirs.'

Memories from the past can remain largely undamaged – and these can be released through attentive friendship. Released from some of the burden of having to store new information when communicating, the person with dementia can find some satisfaction. Conversations need not be long or rushed: ask only one question at a time; key into a person's feelings; allow time for a person to reply; and do not be afraid of silence. All these help to establish good communication.

Professor James argues forcibly that there are viable alternatives to the use of anti-psychotic drugs. 'If the person is comfortable with their familiar old narrative, then they are much more likely to see the necessity for eating, sleeping, going to the toilet, and other vital functions that can be so difficult for carers to orchestrate.'

None of us should be content with a *status quo* in which a reductionist medical model of care has the potential to overlook the person suffering from the condition. People living with dementia need to have their condition reconstructed. If we can redefine the problems of time, memory and history for them, then new solutions can emerge. If, as I suspect, there is a connection and not a discontinuity between the worlds of dementia and those without, then we have been culpable in the past of a hideous sin; that of denying humanity to those who, in their vulnerability, are perhaps most human. This illustrates the central challenge of this book: to understand and affirm that people with dementia may be seen primarily as people – people 'unconditionally held within the love of God', people who retain their personhood until death, though it may be difficult to access.

Before Dame Cicely Saunders died, she wrote to me about my work in caring for the elderly, challenging me to see it as pioneering, as hers was in hospice care in the 1960s and onwards.

I hope the Church will play its part, and share in the challenges and opportunities of those who live in the complex land between remembering and forgetting. Older people are the Churches' natural spiritual constituency; in facing the challenges of dementia we are offered the pastoral opportunity to embrace this experience in all its complexity. Understanding these needs and aspirations can help the Church become inclusive, intelligent, and wise.

Note

1   James, O., *Contented Dementia*, Vermilion, 2008.

List of Contributors

James Woodward
Canon of Windsor.

Kate Read
Executive Director of Dementia Plus – the Dementia Services Development Centre for the West Midlands.

Patricia Higgins
Memory service nurse, Oxleas NHS Foundation Trust.

Richard Allen
Chaplain, South-West London and St George's Mental Health NHS Trust.

Brian Allen
Chaplaincy Team Leader, Newcastle, North Tyneside and Northumberland Mental Health NHS Trust.

Judith Allford
Head of Pastoral Care, Ashford and St Peter's Hospitals NHS Trust.

Margaret Anne Tibbs
A freelance consultant and trainer in dementia care, and a part-time project officer with the Bradford Dementia Group.

John Killick
Associate research Fellow in Communications through the Arts at the Stirling Dementia Services Development Centre.

Gaynor Hammond
Regional tutor for Yorkshire at the Northern Baptist College.

Sally Knocker
Works part-time for NAPA, the National Association for Providers of Activites for Older People.

Katherine Froggatt
Senior Lecturer in the Institute for Health Research, Lancaster University.

Adrian Treloar
Consultant in Old Age Psychiatry and a council member of the Guild of Catholic Doctors.

Margaret Goodall
Methodist Minister in Milton Keynes Circuit, Chaplaincy Adviser, MHA care group.

Beatrice Godwin
Social worker and trainer.

Concise Bibliography of Key Texts

Allen, Brian (ed.), *Religious Practice and People with Dementia*, CCOA, 2002.

CCOA, *Visiting People with Dementia*, CCOA and Methodist Homes, 2001.

CCOA, *Worship for People with Dementia*, CCOA and Methodist Homes, 2001.

Crosskey, Chris, *Older People, Faith and Dementia: Twenty-four Practical Talks for Use in Care Homes*, Leveson Paper No. 7, The Leveson Centre and Church Army, 2004.

Froggatt, Alison and Moffitt, Laraine, 'Spiritual Needs and Religious Practice in Dementia Care' in Marshall, Mary (ed.), *State of the Art in Dementia Care*, CPA, 1997.

Goldsmith, Malcolm, *Dementia, Ethics and the Glory of God*, CCOA Occasional Paper No. 11, CCOA, 1998.

Goldsmith, Malcolm, *In a Strange Land: People with Dementia and the Local Church*, 4M Publications, 2004. Available from 34 Cumberland Street, Edinburgh EH3 6SA.

Hammond, Gaynor and Treetops, Jackie, *The Wells of Life: Moments of Worship with People with Dementia – Suggestions for Action*, Faith in Elderly People, Leeds, 2004. Available from 29 Silverdale Avenue, Guiseley, Yorks LS20 8BD.

Higgins, Patricia and Allen, Richard, *Lighting the Way: Spiritual and Religious Care for Those with Dementia*, Leveson Paper No. 16, The Leveson Centre, 2007.

Killick, John and Allan, Kate, *Communication and the Care of People with Dementia*, Open University Press, 2001.

Murphy, Charles J., *Dementia Care and the Churches: Involving People and Premises*, Dementia Services Development Centre, Stirling, 1997.

Palliative Care for People with Dementia, papers presented at a Leveson seminar, The Leveson Centre, 2005.

Saunders, J., *Dementia: Pastoral Theology and Pastoral Care*, Grove Books, 2002.

Seeing the Person beyond the Dementia, papers presented at a Leveson seminar, 2004, The Leveson Centre.

Shamy, Eileen, *A Guide to the Spiritual Dimension of Care for People with Alzheimer's Disease and Related Dementia*, Jessica Kingsley, 2003.

Treetops, J., *Holy, Holy, Holy: The Church's Ministry for People with Dementia: Suggestions for Action*, Faith in Elderly People, Leeds, 1996. Available from 29 Silverdale Avenue, Guiseley, Yorks LS20 8BD.

Woodward, James, *Valuing Age; Pastoral Ministry with Older People*, SPCK, 2008.

Worship for People with Dementia, MHA and CCOA, 2001.

Appendix:
Further Reading and Resources

Spiritual needs of older people

Airey, Jo et al. (2002) *Frequently Asked Questions on Spirituality and Religion*, CCOA, MHA, Faith in Elderly People.

Jewell, Albert (ed.) (1999) *Spirituality and Ageing*, Jessica Kingsley.

MacKinlay, Elizabeth (2001) *The Spiritual Dimension of Ageing*, Jessica Kingsley.

MacKinlay, Elizabeth (2006) *Spiritual Growth and Care in the Fourth Age*, Jessica Kingsley.

SCOP (2006) *Spiritual Care for Older People: The Extra Dimension*, continuing series of sheets, SCOP.

Wainwright, David (2001) *Being Rather than Doing: A Spirituality of Retirement*, CCOA.

Wray, Martin (2005) *Second Wind: Spirituality and the Second Half of Life* (study course), MHA Care Group

Raising awareness

Bytheway, B. (1995) *Ageism*, Open University Press.

Finney, J. (1992) *Finding Faith Today*, British and Foreign Bible Society.

Green, M. (1990) *Evangelism Through the Local Church*, Hodder and Stoughton.

Slater, R. (1995) *The Psychology of Growing Old*. Open University Press.

Taylor, R. (1996) *Love in the Shadows*, Scripture Union.

Taylor, R. (2004) *Three Score Years and Then? How to Reach Older People for Christ*, available from OUTLOOK Trust Tel. 01494 485222.

Living with loss and change

Counsel and Care (1995) *Last Rights: A Study of How Death and Dying are Handled in Residential Care and Nursing Homes,* Counsel and Care.

A Good Death (2003) papers presented at a Leveson seminar (Leveson Paper No. 4), The Leveson Centre.

A Good Funeral (2006) papers presented at a Leveson seminar (Leveson Paper No. 14), The Leveson Centre.

Missinne, Leo (2004) *Journeying through Old Age and Illness* (Leveson Paper No. 10), The Leveson Centre.

Woodward, James (2005) *Befriending Death,* SPCK.

Woodward, James (2006) *Befriending Illness* (Leveson Paper No. 13), The Leveson Centre.

URC (2002) . . . *A Time to Die: A Resource Pack for Churches,* United Reformed Church.

The ministry of the Church to people living with dementia

Allen, Brian (ed.) (2002) *Religious Practice and People with Dementia,* CCOA.

CCOA (2001) *Visiting People with Dementia,* CCOA and Methodist Homes.

CCOA (2001) *Worship for People with Dementia,* CCOA and Methodist Homes.

Crosskey, Chris (2004) *Older People, Faith and Dementia: Twenty-four Practical Talks for use in Care Homes* (Leveson Paper No. 7), The Leveson Centre and Church Army.

Froggatt, Alison and Moffitt, Laraine (1997) 'Spiritual Needs and Religious Practice in Dementia Care', in Mary Marshall (ed.), *State of the Art in Dementia Care,* CPA.

Goldsmith, Malcolm (1998) *Dementia, Ethics and the Glory of God* (CCOA Occasional Paper No. 11), CCOA.

Goldsmith, Malcolm (2004) *In a Strange Land: People with Dementia and the Local Church,* 4M Publications, available from 34 Cumberland Street, Edinburgh EH3 6SA.

Hammond, Gaynor and Treetops, Jackie (2004) *The Wells of Life: Moments of Worship with People with Dementia, Suggestions for Action,* Faith in Elderly People, Leeds. Available from 29 Silverdale Avenue, Guiseley, Yorkshire LS20 8BD.

Higgins, Patricia and Allen, Richard (2007) *Lighting the Way: Spiritual and Religious Care for those with Dementia* (Leveson Paper No. 16), The Leveson Centre.

Killick, John and Allan, Kate (2001) *Communication and the Care of People with Dementia*, Open University Press.

Murphy, Charles J. (1997) *Dementia Care and the Churches: Involving People and Premises*, Dementia Services Development Centre, Stirling.

Palliative Care for People with Dementia (2005) papers presented at a Leveson seminar, The Leveson Centre.

Saunders, J. (2002) *Dementia: Pastoral Theology and Pastoral Care*, Grove Books.

Seeing the Person Beyond the Dementia, papers presented at a Leveson seminar (2004), The Leveson Centre.

Shamy, Eileen (2003) *A Guide to the Spiritual Dimension of Care for People with Alzheimer's Disease and Related Dementia* (previously published in New Zealand as *More than Body, Brain and Breath*), Jessica Kingsley.

Treetops, J. (1996) *Holy, Holy, Holy: The Church's Ministry for People with Dementia: Suggestions for Action*, Faith in Elderly People, Leeds. Available from 29 Silverdale Avenue, Guiseley, Yorkshire LS20 8BD.

Worship for People with Dementia (2001), MHA and CCOA.